The Coming of the Rain

The Coming of the Rain

The Life of Dr Joe Church

A Personal Account of
Revival in Rwanda

Katharine Makower

Illustrated by Joe Church's granddaughter,

CAROLINE CHURCH

paternoster
press

Paternoster Press is an imprint of Paternoster Publishing,
P.O. Box 300, Carlisle, Cumbria, CA3 0QS, UK
http://www.paternoster-publishing.com

British Library Cataloguing in Publication Data

A catalogue record for this book is available from the
British Library

ISBN 0-85364-968-5

*The illustrations in this book are taken from original drawings
and have been reproduced with the permission of the artist,
Caroline Church.*

Cover Design by Mainstream, Lancaster
Typeset by WestKey Limited, Falmouth, Cornwall
Printed in Great Britain by
Caledonian International Book Manufacturing Limited, Glasgow

Contents

Foreword

Omuggo oguli ewamunno tegugoba ngo *(Luganda)*
*The club at your neighbour's house will not chase away a
menacing leopard at yours*

In writing a foreword to the rounded picture of Dr Joe
Church, and his family, so vividly painted for us in this
biography by Katharine Makower, I am reminded of
this Luganda proverb which encourages us to recognise that
each one of us must encounter the challenge of evil personally, and that we cannot simply rely on the faith of others.

Dr Joe Church in his own autobiography, *Quest for the
Highest, a Diary of the East Africa Revival*, tells the story of
the encounter of two broken worlds bending at the foot
of the Cross of Calvary. There we see how African and
European, black and white, were brought together by
Christ himself living and enthroned in their hearts. We are
told of the tension and heart-searching that marked the
early years of the East African Revival and the remarkable
way in which a division, which could easily have led to a
schism between the staid institutional church and the
revival movement, was healed. But, like the gospel of Luke,
the story is not really complete without a second volume.
Katharine Mokower's biography of Dr Joe Church is, in my
opinion, the second volume of *Quest for the Highest*.

Revival is still the major theme of the book and the story is brought up to date in a masterly way with an account of the tragic events which developed in Rwanda after Joe Church had left. In this biography we are also told of Joe's early years, which along with tales of his intrepid missionary forbears, fill gaps in his own 'first volume' and throw light on his life and work. Katharine Makower has succeeded in reflecting Joe Church to us through the eyes of others, particularly his family. The story is told with honesty, simplicity and transparency. As a child of the East African Revival myself, reading it is like listening to a respected and much loved leader and elder of the Revival telling his story of 'walking in the light'.

My vivid memory of Joe Church is of a doctor and brother in Christ, for ever working too hard 'like a puppy chasing its own tail', always striving for the highest, with Decie by his side reminding him, without saying a word, to nestle in the peace of Christ. He was a faithful preacher of the Gospel, and as a teenager I dearly loved the pictorial images he used. He was a good example to me of how prayer can be victorious and effective when Christians are in fellowship with God and with each other. These special gifts plus his boundless energy, vision and enthusiasm and his eye for detail, shine through the pages of this book loud and clear. The picture that is clearly brought into focus is of a great lover of Jesus Christ.

I am grateful to Katharine Makower for writing this biography to coincide with the centenary of Joe Church's birth. Like his five children, many Ugandans and others will feel a real sense of gratitude for the detailed diaries and photographic records that he kept. Through them we learn how Joe and Decie faced overwhelming challenges and dangers and how they were sorely tried and hard-pressed but never abandoned East Africa. It is this commitment to a people and a country that led all five children to return to Uganda after their graduation in England. Michael helped me buy an Eko guitar and taught me how to play it in my teenage days. John helped me transport Crusader class children in Kampala; Janine helped with cup cakes and banana bread for the Kampala Crusader birthday tea party at Nakasero; Robin advised us which doctor to register with when we arrived in Cambridge; David was to advise me how to re-order the church in Tulse Hill, south London, when I became a vicar.

May the Spirit of truth help, as he did for Joe Church, all who read this book, to forget all else and take the risk of faith which is ready for adventure and looks with patience beyond this world, as we walk with the living Lord Jesus Christ. For the book clearly shows that as we wait upon God, even in earth's desert places, he will give us his vision, and with it all the toil and trouble of the way becomes worthwhile.

St Luke the Apostle's Day, 1998
The Rt Rev Dr John Sentamu
Bishop of Stepney

Preface

It has been a great privilege to write this account of the life of such a dedicated man of God as Dr Joe Church. Rather like a Catherine wheel, he seemed to throw off sparks of enthusiasm in all directions – and the sparks inspired similar enthusiasm in others. The East African revival is sometimes described in terms of flame – the fire of the Holy Spirit – and sometimes, instead, as the refreshing rain. God sends the rain, and it can bring storm and tempest as well as refreshment and new life. In Joe's experience it certainly brought both. Curiously, it was only after the title of the book was chosen that I learnt that Joe Church's Lunyaruanda nickname *Imvura Iaje* actually means 'the coming of the rain'!

I have not given the sources of all my quotations in the course of the narrative, as they would have clogged it up and slowed it down. My main sources are as follows:

- Joe Church's autobiographical account of the East African revival, *Quest for the Highest*, which is based on Joe's own diaries. As he first wrote it, this included five chapters covering his early life, and these unpublished chapters have also been used.
- The Church family diary – a handwritten history of the family compiled by William Church (b. 1805) and going back to 1680.

- The Church family circular letter, 1931–40.
- Circular letter of the Cambridge University Missionary Band (1920), 1922–89.
- An unpublished autobiographical memoir by Dr William Frank Church (Joe's brother Bill) entitled *One Man's Pilgrimage*.
- A remarkable archive collected by Joe Church himself and currently in the care of his son David Church at his home in Richmond, Surrey. This archive includes Joe's diaries, carbon copies of many of the thousands of letters he wrote, letters he received, newspaper cuttings, slides, photographs and much else.
- Meetings and interviews with John, David, Robin, Michael Church and Janine Coleridge, all of whom were most generous, both with information and in sharing with me something of their inner histories. In addition, Michael lent me a box full of letters which his mother Decie wrote to him during the years when he was at school and university in England – an invaluable source of background information, as was his own personal journal of 'rediscovery' of his childhood.

For information about the Moravians, I am indebted to Valerie Barker at the Moravian Church exhibition and information centre, Kings Road, Chelsea.

Special thanks are due to Judith Church, David's wife, who with meticulous scholarship has prepared notes on family members, a family tree, and an exhaustive bibliography. She and David have always had the necessary documents and information at their fingertips and have guided me throughout the project. I could not have written the book without their help.

I am grateful to Jocelyn Murray, who made me a most valuable reading list.

I made contact with many other people – some who were

missionary colleagues of Joe and Decie and who knew them personally, others who followed them at Gahini and elsewhere. Many of these I visited and interviewed, some wrote to me and others I spoke to by telephone. Unfortunately not one of Joe's close African friends and colleagues remains alive to make an up-to-date contribution to the book. Their contribution was in their lives and faith.

I met Joe and Decie once, in their retirement and old age, when I was researching for another book. Joe gave me the copy of *Quest for the Highest* which I have used in writing this account, and I took for this project his dedication, written in 1982, 'To Katharine, with my prayers for the new book she is writing.'

May the dedication of his life inspire many to seek *reality* and 'the highest' in our Christian lives.

Katharine Makower, July 1998

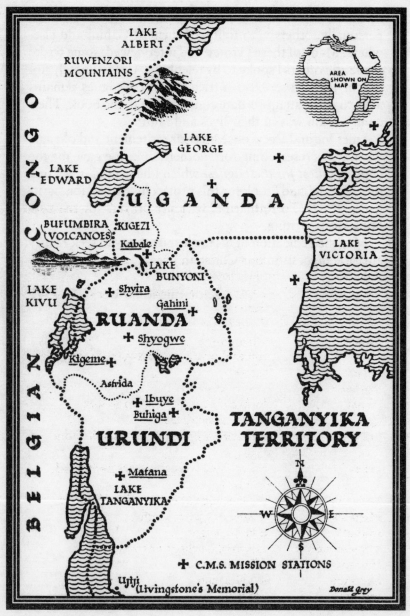

Pre-Independence map, showing the area where Dr Joe Church worked.

Glossary

Lunyaruanda words and phrases (used throughout Rwanda)

Abaka	those on fire (i.e. revival Christians)
Bahutu	Hutu people
Banyaruanda	all people of Ruanda: Bahutu, Batutsi and Batwa
Batutsi	Tutsi people
bazungu	white people
bintu	things (literally) or luggage when travelling
ibigori	maize
ibijumba	sweet potatoes
inama	local chief's council or leadership consultation group
isaa munani	2 o'clock teaching time – literally hour eight
kazu	prayer hut, or small prayer meeting of leaders
Lunyaruanda	the language of the people of Ruanda
Mugabikazi	Ruandan Queen Mother
Muhutu	a Hutu person
Muraho mwese!	Greeting – hello, everyone
Mututsi	a Tutsi person
muzungu	a white man
umusaza	old man

Luganda words and phrases (used by the Baganda people of Uganda)

balokole	saved ones (i.e. revival Christians)
Kabaka	King of Buganda
obukulu	*clericalism*
tukutendereza Yesu	we praise you Jesus
zukuka	awake

Note on spelling of the word *Rwanda*:

Pre-independence   Ruanda
Post-independence   Rwanda
Mission name, both pre- and post-independence:
Ruanda Mission, Church Missionary Society
Mission name from 1990:   Mid-Africa Ministry (CMS)
Both Ruanda and Urundi became independent on 1 July 1962, when the name Urundi was changed to Burundi.

Prologue: Going Home

The road from Goma to Kisenyi began to fill with people walking, often silently, but determinedly, towards Rwanda, their meagre possessions hastily bundled together, carried on their heads, after two years in exile in neighbouring Zaire. Many of the younger children were now returning to a country they had never known.

While the international community deliberated on how best to become involved with aid, or military intervention, in a situation seemingly too complex to understand, Africa had once again started to resolve the situation in its own way. The murderous gangs which had held these families in their grip of fear in the refugee camps had now dissolved into the Congo forests to the west, leaving behind evidence of their plans to re-invade Rwanda with arms, which along with humanitarian aid from the Western World had been sustaining them.

The disciplined young soldiers welcoming the returning refugees at the border seemed to give a new sense of stability and hope. Many of these young soldiers were themselves strangers in their own land, their families having been driven out into refugee camps in Uganda at the time of Independence in the 1960s.

Migrations of people over these artificial borders, set up by colonial administrators in the last century, have been going on for hundreds of years. The original inhabitants were probably the diminutive Batwa Pygmies, who had learnt to live by hunting and gathering in the dense rain-forest which still covers much of equatorial Africa, including parts of Rwanda. The Bahutu, with their skills in subsistence farming evidenced in the terraced hillsides which support rich crops of maize (*ibigori*), sweet potatoes (*ibijumba*), beans and bananas, had probably migrated originally from the west. Later, some three hundred years ago, came the Batutsi from the north, driving their herds of long-horned cattle over the open savannah land that lies in the rain shadow of the Mountains of the Moon. Their striking appearance, and similarity to the Masai and other nomadic herdsmen tribes that inhabit the Great Rift Valley grassland areas of central Africa, suggest a common ancestry from the ancient civilizations of the upper Nile. Finally, within living memory for some, came the white man.

We too have walked that Goma road, but as children in a land that we thought was home. So where and what is home? When in Africa our family talked of home leave in England, but when in England, even still, there is the home-sickness for the Africa we knew. Our relationship with Africa was not, however, the same as that of our parents. They were pioneers who settled for a time in Africa while re-maining firmly rooted, with supportive families, in England. Our roots were in the fertile hills of Ruanda and Kigezi and in the wild sage-scented bush country, alive with the sound of familiar birds and animals. It was many years later that we had to dig deep to discover our own roots in England.

Glimpses of newsreel pictures of the refugees on the road to Kisenyi provided instant reminders of the wonderful quality of that part of the world. Particularly memorable were the camping holidays near the sandy beach (the name Kisenyi means 'the place of sand'), with the dramatic backdrop of the volcanic Bufumbira mountains lighting up the night with firework displays of lava. After one of the larger eruptions we once watched the relentless flow of molten lava blocking the road, on its way to Lake Kivu, and the clouds of hissing steam rising where it entered the water. We even ventured up onto the hardened crust to see the red-hot flow, deep in the cracks beneath our feet, and some were even bold enough to swim in the heated lake water. On other occasions we explored the extensive network of underground tunnels, formed long ago from earlier eruptions, where molten rock had engulfed former river courses. So this landscape of wonderful variety and beauty was itself created out of violent movements in the earth's surface. The slow drift of the African continental plate resulted, many millions of years ago, in the dramatic crack in the earth's crust which we call the Great Rift Valley. Extending from the north through the Jordan valley in Israel to the central African plateau and down to Southern Africa, it has left a chain of volcanic mountains, some now long extinct and snow covered; and lakes, some baked by the sun into soda pans, others, filled with fresh water, which have spilled over to feed the great rivers which flow into the Atlantic Ocean to the west, the Mediterranean to the north and the Indian Ocean to the south. Rwanda can thus be described as the watershed of Africa. This too is the land of the mountain gorilla. Our father, reputed to be the first to scale Sabinio, one of the higher peaks, described how he could only progress in the dense rainforest by following the gorilla tracks, never knowing what he was likely to meet. Today, much of the forest has gone and the banana plantations, which creep ever higher into the mountains, provide easy pickings for the remaining gorillas, leading inevitably to conflict with the expanding human population.

So much in Africa depends on rain. When it arrives late, crops wither in the ground and starvation follows. At other times it comes with such dramatic force that crops are washed off the hillsides and the land is left bare and eroded, bridges are carried away and roads become impassable. One of our earliest, and most vivid, childhood memories is the coming of the rain at Gahini. At first the rustling of the breeze in the high gum trees, and the rippling of the lake, would suggest that the dry season was at last over. Then came the sweet smell of the cool raindrops on dusty earth, and the welcoming chorus of songbirds. Finally, with a roar on the hot corrugated iron roofs, the rain would be on us and we brothers would strip and run naked in the refreshing deluge.

Security was not at that time an apparent problem. The precautions we now take for granted in England did not seem to be necessary. In Ruanda and later at Kabale in Uganda we would sleep on the veranda, protected only by mosquito nets. Bicycles and furniture left outside did not instantly disappear. Far from the nearest town we had become almost self-sufficient. Our mother created flourishing fruit-and-vegetable gardens, with at least six varieties of bananas, in the lakeside plantation. Our father never threw anything away and kept several old bathtubs full of redundant objects on the back veranda, knowing that a good rummage would inevitably reveal the perfect component for some essential repair work one day. The household staff were trusted completely, and became part of our extended family. In fact, our first words were in Lunyaruanda, being our means of communication with the African girl who looked after us while our mother was otherwise occupied in mission work in support of our father.

One realizes that so much in Africa has changed and yet so much continues as it has for centuries. As children, and later as teenagers and young adults, we were able to see the same world that our parents experienced, but from a different perspective. We are fortunate that our father kept detailed diaries and photographic records, and it is in reading these diaries and letters that we realize how close we had been to the almost overwhelming challenges that he and our mother had to face, and yet how protected we had been from it all.

We all returned: John as doctor in charge of Gahini Hospital and later as Lecturer in orthopaedics at Makerere University in Uganda; David as an architect involved in construction of schools, hospitals, churches and public buildings, including the Bank of Uganda Headquarters in Kampala; Robin as doctor in charge of Kabarole Hospital at Fort Portal, in Uganda; Michael as a doctor with Save the Children Fund involved in health education; and Janine as a physiotherapist married to a doctor in the Uganda Government medical service. We had all in different ways been affected by the impact of our parents' example and teaching, but returned at a time when dramatic changes were taking place in the whole of Africa.

John, David, Robin, Michael and Janine. Children of Joe and Decie Church.

1

1895–1916: A Rural Idyll

In September 1895, far removed from the enterprise, decadence and fogs of late Victorian London, the Rev Edward Joseph Church was appointed as rector of Burrough Green, a sleepy Cambridgeshire village of some four hundred people south of Newmarket, where the main event of the week was the leisurely cricket match on the village green. His father and two brothers ran a successful family firm, Church and Sons, from an office directly under the Monument in the City of London, importing dried fruits and sugar and supplying the navy victualling yard at Deptford, but he felt called to minister in the church. A month after his arrival, on 16 October, he married Florence Edith Badger, daughter of the Rev William Collins Badger, a Hebrew scholar from Birmingham who at that time was rector of Bressingham in Norfolk. Edward was an earnest young man, with a face both sensitive and determined; Florence was good-looking and practical, with clearly defined features and lively intelligent eyes.

At the end of a short lane, leading off the green, stands the ancient, grey-stone parish church with its low tower. From its uncluttered interior, with white walls, oak pews and brick floor, the large plain glass windows link the worshipper with the quiet beauty outside, tall trees harbouring rooks' nests swaying under the wide East Anglian sky. Just beyond the church is the roomy Victorian rectory surrounded by fields and trees and here, in the upstairs bedroom with roses climbing round the window, all ten of Edward and Florence's children were born.

They worked hard, struggled to make ends meet and to provide for their large and lively brood, but for the best part of the next half-century Edward and Florence remained within a small area of Cambridgeshire, and their lives, despite the Great War, were preserved to some extent in an Edwardian and interwar idyll. The wider world and its rapid changes seemed barely to touch them. Serene and secure in their faith, they passed this security on to their children as they sought to share their belief in a loving God with the people around them. And yet both in earlier generations of the family and among their children as they grew up were those, equally sure of their faith, who covered thousands of miles to reach remote peoples with the message of Jesus Christ. One of these pioneers was Edward and Florence's eldest son Joe, born on 10 August 1899, and a study of his story reflects something of the 'tide in the affairs of men' and of God's hand guiding it.

During their 21 years in Burrough Green, Florence bore Edward ten children: Violet (born 1896), William Christian who died in infancy, John Edward (Joe), Mary, Margaret (Daisy), William (Bill), Howard, Christine (Wizz), George and the youngest, Elizabeth (Betty) who was born in 1914. Although they were far from well off, their childhood was happy and free in the rambling house with its sunny lawn stretching away to the 'ha-ha' which cut the garden off from the paddock beyond. Edward's stipend was small and he hesitated to demand the little extra rental which the tenants of his glebe land were supposed to pay him. But Florence worked hard to render the family self-sufficient, and with a cow, pigs, hens and a well-stocked vegetable garden, orchard and beehives, the large family were always well fed. They had pets too – ponies, a donkey, beloved dogs. For some years their uncle's 'horseless carriage' was the only car that occasionally came to the village. A major sadness of those years was Wizz's attack of polio which necessitated her wearing a leg-iron, but they all helped her along and didn't let her feel left out. Life at home was fun, with tennis on the lawn and swimming in the pond. There was much practical joking and considerable freedom within a structure of loving discipline. The children all started their education at the small charity school nearby on the green. Edward took a keen interest in this school and organized the raising of money to add a new infants' room. He was also a good cricketer and supporter of the local cricket club. Florence was known far and wide for her tennis, her energy and her kindness. In spite of her many domestic duties she established a branch of the Mothers' Union, taught in the Sunday school, and organized working parties to make clothes for a leprosy hospital in China. Joe described his childhood:

We all grew up to run wild in the fields in any weather, to ride ponies, to climb trees, to shoot rabbits and to arrange tennis parties. But our education suffered. Our governesses did not last long nor could they cope with the isolation or, we imagine, with the Church family! We were two-and-a-half miles from the nearest railway station and it took most of the day to catch a train in the pony cart and to get back walking up the hills. I had to go to the village school where I worked at the back at a new single desk that I suppose had to be specially made for the parson's son. All ages and both sexes seemed to be taught together in the one room. There was a definite 'vernacular' that had to be learnt in order to communicate, and a few raw country folk and children spoke a dialect of Cambridgeshire English that was hardly intelligible. They used to rag the parson's son but I made up for it by playing cricket with them on the village green, keeping wicket with a pair of my father's leather gloves.

When he was eleven and still barely able to write, Joe was sent to the junior school of St Lawrence College, Ramsgate, a school they could afford because for sons of clergy there were practically no fees. He was teased unmercifully about his village accent, his rough clothes, his dry skin, his stutter. Externally cheerful, he battled with various worries on his own. Hearing the Bible story of the man with the withered hand expounded in the school chapel, he would look at his own hands in winter, rough and chapped, wondering if they too were withering. His stuttering sometimes provoked laughter, but an understanding godmother, his mother's sister, would sit with him when he was at home, taking his hand and teaching him to breathe properly and quietly until his words flowed again.

He learnt from these experiences the need for sympathetic tactful help, a lesson which he was to draw on to help others in Africa later on.

In the holidays, life at Burrough Green continued much as before. Joe and Bill roamed the countryside with their shared airgun, bagging rabbits and pigeons for the pot. Once though, coming home from one of his favourite tramps round the hedgerows shortly before returning to school in September, Joe saw a huge cock-pheasant looking down at him from a tree, its body silhouetted against the sunset. Throwing caution to the winds, he shot it down and smoothed out its beautiful tail feathers. What an addition to his trophies on the wall of the potting shed! He ran home proudly to show his father, who was not impressed. Although the bird was in their own paddock, it belonged to the Squire and to him it must go. The Squire had a good laugh and warned Joe never to do such a thing again. 'Rector, take it home and roast it and have a good meal with the family!' he kindly added. But despite the pleas of the family and with the loyal support of his wife, Edward insisted that, down at the bottom of the garden by lamplight, Joe solemnly dig a grave. He was allowed to keep some tail feathers; then they buried the pheasant and Edward's sensitive conscience was at peace.

Discipline was firm but consistent. Very rarely did Florence have to fall back on the last line of defence – sending a child to their father's study. Never did Edward have to chastise any of his children. How was it done? Joe described it like this:

I look back at our dining room with my father at his place at one end and my mother serving at the other end of the table. We generally sat down ten or twelve in the holidays. There was plenty of fun and chatter and we all knew my father's funny stories which he would try out on our guests. Girls of my mother's era learned 'charm' and we loved her graciousness, but she was the disciplinarian of the family. She used to stand up towards the end of a meal and tap the table with a spoon and call us all to stop talking and listen to her 'public notice' as she called it. This became a family ritual: 'Muddy boots left lying about the hall'; 'Some of you were rude to Joe Missen (the gardener) – this must stop'; unkindness to animals was anathema, as we knew by the tone of her voice. Finally, 'No picking of strawberries without permission. Now you can all get down.' There was one thing that we all knew from infancy, that was the grip of my mother's hand when she meant what she said and it had to be obeyed. This went with a certain tightening of the lips and a change in her voice. If that grip of my mother's hand had wavered or if she had stopped to plead with us, 'Don't you know Mummy's tired?', we would have lost confidence in her and that vital thing security would have gone. If we disobeyed we knew we must be led off to our room for a time. It was the beginning of learning that 'the wages of sin is death'. It was the beginning of the understanding of grace and forgiveness. We had another family way of ending the punishment. We would all look at Mother at the end of the table and try to make her laugh. Slowly her face would quiver into a smile and the whole table would break into laughter and fun again with Father joining in at the far end.

Her children all loved and trusted her. Bill, later to spend much of his life in Africa, recalls his first memory: 'Walking in the garden with my mother in the evening, aged four. A flock of rooks flew overhead. "Where are they going?" I asked. "Home," she replied.' 'I cannot understand', he commented years later, 'why this simple memory has persisted.' The Church family's developing story throws light on the joy and the pain of this concept of *home*.

Joe described his father as

abnormally sensitive – a trait I think he passed on to me. He would have a sleepless night if he had been unkind to one of the parishioners or hurt somebody's feelings. I never remember him getting angry, but he had times of depression and worry, especially over the financial burdens that hung over us like a cloud. He also had the family trait of 'going quiet'. That was where my mother came in with her amazing gift of comfort and encouragement. She would say, 'Ed dear, I want to show you something in the garden.' Out they would go, arm in arm, down to the vegetable garden which was my father's special care (the flowers were hers) and as they walked between the box edging the worries would be given to God and we would hear his hearty laugh again.

Joe moved on to the senior school at St Lawrence. His copy of the School Register, half eaten by African ants, shows that he began to distinguish himself at hockey and shooting. Despite Zeppelin raids, when a letter home records 'tophole fun in the funk-hole (bomb shelter)', his academic work improved. His father had high hopes that Joe would follow in his footsteps and become a clergyman, and had entered him for Trinity College, Cambridge. With little enthusiasm, Joe studied classics at school with this in view. The school was evacuated to Chester because of the raids. Meanwhile, at home the country idyll was about to come to an end.

2

1917–1919: Merry-go-round

One evening in 1916 as the nights were drawing in, Edward sat alone in the quietness of his study, looking into the fire. He often retreated there from the rough and tumble of the family. Now he sat deep in thought, an open letter on his lap, which if acted upon would mean change for them all. When Florence came in, eager for a few minutes' peace at the end of a busy day, he showed it to her. Watching her expression as she read it, he wondered afresh how it was that the decisions he came to were always the ones that his wife agreed with. A skilful general who knew just how to lead from the rear, she had a way of conveying wisdom and decisiveness to him without his realizing it. She handed the letter back and waited for him to speak.

It was from the Archdeacon: 'The living of St Andrew the Less, Cambridge, has just become vacant and I feel that you are the man to take it. Will you let me know, when you have had time to consider it, whether you feel called to this task. I will not deceive you, it is an arduous one.' St Andrew the Less, or the Abbey Church as it is also known, was a very old church, built in the thirteenth century by the Canons of Barnwell Priory. In the nineteenth century the population of its large parish grew, the church proved much too small, and several more churches were built to serve the area. It was one of these, Christ Church in the Newmarket Road, which took over as the parish church when the Abbey Church fell into disrepair and could no longer be used. So in fact Edward was being invited to minister at Christ Church in a large parish of eleven thousand people in the poor and industrial part of Cambridge – a completely different situation from Burrough Green.

For both of them it would be a wrench. They had been happy at Burrough Green and had brought up all their children there. But Edward summed up the thought in both their minds. If this was a call from God, they must be prepared to obey. And Florence encouraged him, 'Dearest, if the Archdeacon has asked you, he must know that there is a greater need in Cambridge and that you are the man to meet it – with God's help. I *shall* miss the country, our dear people here, our lovely garden – and the animals; but', and her face brightened, 'of course we will have a garden there too, and it will be a great advantage for the dear children with their schooling.' Florence always saw the bright side where she could. The next day, Edward posted off his letter of acceptance. It was entirely in character that neither had discussed what the stipend for the new appointment would be.

Sadly, the cow and the ponies had to be sold. Daisy ran weeping down the road with Taffy the foal all the way to his new home, and she kept a tuft of his hair as a memento long afterwards in her Bible. Soon, on a freezing January day in 1917, a line of horses and wagons stood in the drive, the breath of the animals rising like smoke in the cold still air, and the solid and somewhat battered furniture from the rectory was stowed on board. With Edward, Florence, Betty, George and Wizz in the pony-cart and the others on bicycles, they headed for the railway junction and so to Cambridge.

Their new home was an imposing Georgian vicarage opposite the church in the Newmarket road. The huge, cold, empty rooms echoed hollowly to their footsteps. Betty, the youngest, overcome by the gloom and the cold and the unfamiliarity of it all, sat forlornly in the middle of the floor while the others found kindling and coal in an outhouse and managed to light the kitchen range. As they were clearing up after a picnic lunch on the floor in front of the welcome blaze, a telegraph boy brought a message to say that the horses pulling the furniture carts had been unable to get up Six Mile Bottom, one of the few hills in Cambridgeshire, because of the ice. Florence managed to arrange for various friends and relations around Cambridge to put them up, and eventually, two weeks later, the furniture arrived and they moved in. As the children left their various hostesses, there were sighs of relief all round: 'Such *nice* children, but – a little rough, you know, and so lively,' was how one battered hostess expressed the general feeling. And things in the vicarage continued to be lively as Bill and Howard, when they weren't at school, engaged in various crusades, pelting bookies cycling past to the Newmarket races with green potatoes, or catapulting a stone at the screeching mezzo-soprano practising by the open window across the road.

For Joe, the eldest, however, horizons were beginning to widen. In January 1918, the last year of the war, he was chosen among the senior boys at St Lawrence College to train for a commission in the Tank Corps. Travelling down to London in the train he couldn't believe his good fortune: no more 'swot'; his bed in the dormitory would be empty that night. But looking back many years later, he commented:

One gets restless when running away from God. Any fixed job or routine becomes prisonlike and we jump at any change. Public school life with its house-match battles, friendships, Bisley rifle shooting, and piles of toast on the study floor made by the 'fags' was on the whole enjoyable, yet the prisonlike feeling remained. The real bondage lies in the soul that has not yet found freedom.

Daily life for many people is like a trip on the merry-go-round at a fair. You sit on one of the brightly coloured horses and race round and round, just having time now and again to wave to friends who are watching you from their horses, getting nowhere, and all to the sound of churned-out music. Leaving St Lawrence and entering the army was in many ways simply changing from one merry-go-round to another. At school some of us would start the day by sliding down the central staircase of the tower at the last possible moment to dive into a cold bath in the basement. There was an unofficial record for the fastest time from the top floor to the basement. Then followed roll-call, 'swot' hour after hour, dashing from one classroom to another with a huge pile of books under one's arms, and then exams. The backdrop was the smell of the classroom, chalk, ink, notebooks, games lockers, Corps boots, the chapel and the dormitories. In any odd moments we dreamt of holidays.

In the army the merry-go-round changed. It was reveille to a bugle, blankets folded, boot cleaning, button polishing, inspection on the parade ground, standing at attention not moving an eyelid, marching up and down, then back to the hangars to fight with guns, machinery and engines – and all to the background of sweat, khaki clothes, marching feet, loud voices and saluting. Then at night exhausted sleep except for those who delighted in capping each other's dirty stories. I managed to survive, and in the spring of 1918 was duly posted to the Tank Corps officer cadet training camp at Winchester on Hazeley Down. My officer's uniform was admired by my five sisters on my short leave home to Cambridge. They all wanted a brass button with a tank on it to make into a brooch, which was the fashion in wartime England.

Dark haired and handsome, sturdily built and now sporting a moustache which he kept all his life, Joe was becoming an increasingly dashing and glamorous figure to his sisters, especially later when he acquired a motorbike. He was especially kind to his youngest sister, Betty, who missed him and her other brothers away at school. He would take her for rides in his sidecar, her hair blowing in the wind, and one magical day he brought her a puppy of her own, which became her dearest friend.

Joe threw himself into the new life, including the many opportunities for sport. It was springtime, and the lilac and laburnum of the Winchester gardens seemed to bring new hope as the last year of World War I lingered on. One evening through the lighted door of one of the huts he spotted a soldier kneeling beside his bed saying his prayers. 'I often wonder who that lad was, for his lone witness was used to remind me of my mother's prayers as she said goodnight to us, and to warn me that I was slipping away and forgetting it all in the excitement of army life. Yet somehow it annoyed me. I didn't want to be reminded.'

In September, aged just nineteen, he was commissioned as Second Lieutenant. On 1 November he started serving as acting assistant Adjutant with the Twentieth Tank Battalion at Bovington in Dorset, and ten days later, on 11 November 1918 came news of the end of the war. Joe faced a choice, whether to apply to continue in the army, or to comply with his father's hopes and go to Trinity College, Cambridge, with a view to becoming a clergyman. He applied for a two-year extension in the army: 'Christmas came and a long weekend at home with all the family – thirteen around the long table – and I broke the news that I was staying on in the army. There was immediate agreement.' And as Joe commented many years later, 'What a wonderful thing it is to have parents who trust one implicitly in youthful decisions like this.'

Despite, and indeed grateful for the temperance pledge that his mother had got them all to sign, Joe continued to enjoy army life with its challenges, friendships, sport and cross-country runs. In particular, he and a fellow officer discovered a new interest – sailing. With the help of a second-hand motorbike they found a small sailing dinghy for hire in Poole Harbour, and then, as Joe described:

There opened up to us the most wonderful new world of experience. We learned the tides and the half-tides, the changing sandbanks, the cries of the seabirds, the tide-race in and out of the harbour mouth that was almost impossible to sail against in any wind. We made our own rules, not realizing that we were making them for our own personal lives: never stop for the weather; if you get into trouble, you must get yourself out of it; and the 'yard an hour' principle: if you can only make a yard an hour against wind and tide, don't give up. We sailed all day on Sundays and hid from each other the blank space in our hearts called religion.

In fact, Joe was becoming more and more conscious of a deep spiritual emptiness. Often on a Sunday evening, his face still stinging with the salt from the day's sailing, he would go into one of the churches in Bournemouth, avoiding the long service which he remembered all too well from his childhood, but slipping in at the back just to hear the sermon, looking for a reality which eluded him. He tried several churches in this way, only to slip out again disappointed and, turning up the collar of his thick overcoat, walk out to listen to the sea. He was uncertain about his future too. He needed to talk to someone, and chose Dr Alex Wood, tutor of first-year medical students at Emmanuel College, Cambridge, and a friend of his father's. Why did he not talk to his father? 'My father was absent-minded. People loved his visits and his hearty laugh and his gracious manners, but to us children he was far away and too shy to speak with us intimately. This made us bear our burdens alone, especially our problems of adolescence.' Joe tells this story in illustration:

Once in the school holidays, when my mother had finished praying with me and saying good night up in my small top room, I asked her about a certain sex expression that was bandied around at school. The result was rather alarming for me. She hastily kissed me good night and hurried down to my father. Then I heard the study door open and the slow heavy footsteps of my father coming up the carpeted stairs. He came in and quietly walked up and down my room beside my bed in the dark saying nothing. I wondered what I had done wrong. Then he very quietly said something like this: 'John (I was always John to him, but my school nickname Joe was used by the rest of the family), there is a text in the Bible that you may find helpful. It is this, "Know ye not that your body is the temple of the Holy Ghost" '. Then he slipped out and went downstairs again.

So it was to Dr Alex Wood in Cambridge that Joe went and asked whether it might be possible to switch and read medicine at Emmanuel instead of Classics at Trinity: 'I've always been keen on science subjects. I know it will mean hard work, but I don't mind that.' With Dr Wood's encouragement, he now had to broach the matter with his father. At the last moment of his stay, he stood with his parents on the front drive of the vicarage waiting for the taxi.

My mother was looking at her beloved standard roses and my father was taking his presentation gold watch in and out of his waistcoat pocket as he always did when he was waiting for something. I broke the news to them and told them what Dr Wood had said. My father said nothing against my plea, and my mother simply stated that she had always felt that a doctor's profession should be classed at the top with that of a clergyman, but second to it! The taxi came and my father accompanied me as he generally did to the station. He was getting very worried about the education of all his children. The post-war slump had hit the family business in London and it was going into liquidation. All our money had been lost. My two brothers would have to leave school early. I had often watched my mother and father late at night pondering over their bank books trying to decide which of the remaining stocks and shares they could sell in order to keep their large family going. So, humanly speaking, as we shook hands at the station and my father said, 'God bless you, John', I knew full well that there would be little chance of my getting up to Cambridge; the winds of adversity were blowing too strong.

3

1920–1922: Reality

One of Lloyd George's new initiatives for post-war Britain found its way into the Tank Corps CO's office. It was an OHMS circular stating that any student who had interrupted his studies to serve his country could apply for a grant to continue. Straightaway Joe's application forms went in, backed by his CO and 'winged on their way by the hand of God'. In the meantime Joe was beginning to read science and medical textbooks on his own and finding them more and more interesting. He also did a six-week premedical course at Oxford – a special educational refresher course arranged for army men. Two big hurdles remained if he was to start his medical studies at Emmanuel that October: how to get out of the final army year to which he was committed, and how to find the necessary funds. Soon both problems were solved: the first, by another OHMS circular allowing for demobilization in extenuating circumstances, and the second, a few weeks after term began, by the arrival of the grant for which he had applied, covering almost all fees and tuition expenses for the study of medicine for five years. Edward, who hadn't dared to hope for this, was delighted.

For the third time I settled into a new round of intense activity, that of a medical student at Cambridge. It was still the same merry-go-round as before. Games came first – furious hockey. My 'digs' were at home, my study being in a biggish room on the first floor. Here I retreated, hanging my school caps around the room, smoking with my friends but skilfully avoiding all contact with my father's parish activities. My mother used to call up to the window to see if I would come to parish functions, but she gave it up. I had made up my mind that we must go different ways. I had been especially warned by some friends to keep clear of the Cambridge Inter-Collegiate Christian Union – the CICCU. If I met one of them, especially any I had known at school, I would dash past as quickly as possible on my bicycle or go another way.

Students in those days were more prone to pranks than to protest, and Joe was often in the thick of them. He recalled:

Our house too became the centre of a certain amount of parish gaiety. My eldest sister, Violet, was like an extra curate to my father. She could arrange a tennis party, a picnic or a Sunday school outing in no time. We had singing lessons, and dancing lessons too in the evenings when we took up the carpet in the large drawing room and invited friends in to dance. We were a big family and my mother and father allowed us much freedom, but it was the way of emptiness and worldliness for me and I grew more and more hungry for real life. I spent much spare time 'hotting up' my motorcycle. The thing to do was to fit a long exhaust pipe that made a sound like the deep notes of an organ. We would work on it opposite my father's study window on the front drive. I never remember him complaining. Then we roared up the Newmarket Road to try it out.

It was nearly May Week in 1920, and some of my old school-friends were planning to take a party of students to help with a children's beach mission at Whitby in Yorkshire in the summer vacation. As they planned, my name kept coming into their minds and they prayed for my conversion and invited me to join them. I tried every possible excuse, but eventually agreed. Towards the end of August I set off. It was a long journey on my motorbike and I slept in a haystack on the way, little knowing that this journey was to be the end of my long search for the way to God.

About midday I found myself on the cliff-top in Whitby looking at the sea and sands below, beginning to get that 'new boy' feeling and wondering why on earth I had come. Satan was having his last battle for my soul. I caught sight of a red banner with CSSM [Children's Special Service Mission] on it in big letters standing in the sand, a little crowd of children and some undergraduates in flannels carrying a portable harmonium up the zigzag path in the cliffs. It was terrifying. I thought of running away and heading for Scotland. Anything to get away! But at that moment a remarkable thing happened. The first two or three students – and especially a certain John Melly who had won the MC in France at the age of seventeen and later the George Cross in Abyssinia where he was to give his life – spotted me and ran to welcome me. 'Joe, we've been waiting for you. Thank goodness you've come,' they said. 'We need your help with sand-hockey this afternoon.' The love of God had run to meet me and it had run me to earth! This was what I had been looking for at school and in the army when I slipped in to the back of those cold churches. This was reality.

Joe had always loved children. He began to give the boys rides on the back of his motorbike, swimming with them and organizing treasure hunts. He also began to listen to the talks given from the Bible as they sat together on the beach, and finally one day as he prayed the prayer of one of the songs they sang, his eyes were opened:

Cleanse me from my sin, Lord,
Put thy power within, Lord,
Take me as I am, Lord,
And make me all thine own.
Keep me day by day, Lord,
Underneath thy sway, Lord,
Make my heart thy palace
And thy royal throne.

He had found the One who had been standing, knocking patiently at the door of his heart and life for so long. And great was the rejoicing of his friends. A few days later as they were packing up to leave, something else happened which was to have far-reaching effects. A boy of sixteen, son of a Yorkshire landowner, who had been feeling a little out of things at the beach mission, came and talked to Joe, and Joe was able to lead him to his new saviour, Jesus Christ. This made him realize the special needs of older boys like this and led to the idea of holding a cruise for them on the Norfolk Broads in the Easter holidays – the start of the famous 'Walrus' cruises, which still continue.

Back at home in Cambridge, the first challenge was to tell his parents of his decision. He had made a promise to God that he would speak at the very first parish meeting that took place, and to his horror it turned out to be the Mothers' meeting, the last possible occasion at which the parson's wayward son would want to speak. He bravely saw it through, and 'the joy of testimony came as a seal from

God to me'. Afterwards he walked home with his mother. She couldn't speak – 'There was no need. We knew those rather special times in the family when Mother got a lump in her throat and a small lace handkerchief would appear from some mysterious pocket to wipe away a tear.'

In October, after a family holiday on a clinker-built yacht on the Broads, Joe began his second year of medical studies. Puzzlingly, he developed a sharp pain in his right side and a severe cough, so debilitating that he was dropped from the college first XI hockey team and lost his opportunity of a longed-for 'blue'. Twice that autumn he coughed up blood, and the dreaded word 'tuberculosis' forced itself into his mind. On the second occasion, lying in bed at night battling with fear and rebellion, he prayed something like this: 'O Lord Jesus, I gave my life to you at Whitby and now I am yours for ever. I have begun to tell others about you, but what is the good of it if now I am to be ill with a chronic disease which will only be an extra expense to my parents and a worry for everyone?' As he listened, very conscious of God's presence and love, it seemed that he was being asked for something more. It seemed that God was allowing this testing for a special purpose. Out of this moment of crisis was drawn a greater commitment, and Joe promised total surrender to his new Lord, even to going anywhere in the world as a missionary, claiming in faith the victorious Christian life and revival, if God on his part would cure him then and there.

Convinced that God had healed him, the next day Joe asked his parents if the best medical specialist in the university could examine him for his cough, without mentioning the haemorrhages. The specialist came, and found no indication of anything more than bronchitis. By the end of term Joe was fit and back in the Emmanuel hockey team. Years later a radiographer carrying out a routine chest X-ray noticed some old scarring, almost certainly due to past TB, and Joe told him what he had asked God to do for him and of his promise in return that had led him to give his life as a missionary in Africa.

Joe became an active member of the CICCU, learning to study the Bible systematically, following its great themes through from beginning to end using the Scofield chain reference Bible: 'I had never imagined that there could be such a thrill in tracing the great truths through the inspired writings of the Word of God. It was a new world which I entered with relish, as I began to know also a new fellowship, something deeper than the army and even than one's own family.' He studied another book that was very popular in the CICCU at that time, *How to Live the Victorious Life* by an Unknown Christian. Later he often met the 'Unknown Christian', Dr A.E. Richardson. Joe commented later: 'It might be said that Dr Richardson's book on the victorious life was to Cambridge University what Law's *Serious Call to a Devout and Holy Life* was to both John Wesley and George Whitefield at Oxford', and he quoted the editor of *The Life of Faith*'s comment on the book: 'It proclaims the glorious fact that victory may and ought to mark the daily life and witness of God's children – not in a dim and distant future but here and now . . . in the throb and bustle of life, in the trials and temptations, the losses and sorrows.'

He was also introduced to the challenge and thrill of youth work, and found himself thinking about the poorer boys whom he had hardly noticed before, milling about the streets in his father's parish. He started a Bible class in the vicarage for some of them on Sunday afternoons: 'With my army days still so vivid when I had wandered about on cold Sunday nights trying to find Life, I tried to bring the love of God to these teenage boys. We learned together because I too was being helped in that vicarage Bible class.' Joe felt that his new life was opening up like the turning of the pages of a book – an exciting book, with an unseen hand bringing

'God's surprises'. Although his father had some reservations about the CICCU, things were changing too at the vicarage. Joe's undergraduate friends would drop in on Sunday afternoons after preaching in the open air on Parker's Piece or teaching in the Jesus Lane Sunday school. It was open house as an endless supply of bread and butter and cake would come up in the lift from the basement kitchen where everyone gave a hand to Joe's sisters. Although at first they were puzzled by Joe's new seriousness, gradually, one by one his brothers and sisters too turned to Jesus Christ in living faith. Dancing and Joe's smoking faded out very soon, but life was as much fun as ever with musical evenings and games. Florence took in student lodgers to help make ends meet, but even so, Bill and Howard had to leave school early. Bill had a go at the merchant navy, Howard worked for a while in the family business. Both eventually studied at Cambridge, Bill doing medicine and Howard heading for ordination. Eventually each of the five girls married Cambridge graduates. After refusing several suitors, Violet married Kenneth Turner, a slightly surprised railway engineer who hadn't realized that the advertised lodgings he applied for were in a vicarage. They stayed on in Cambridge, but Mary and her husband the Rev Rupert Penn went as missionaries to South India, and a few years later Daisy and her husband Dick Schor headed for South America. As the family gradually dispersed, the parents' wish that their family links should be maintained and cherished was met in part by a circular letter which travelled the world and was added to in the far-flung places where they went. The letters were written, after the first few rounds, in a series of strongly covered exercise books, which continued to circulate until fear of their being destroyed by Second World War submarines ended the venture.

But for the present in 1921, for Joe life was full. In April the first Broads cruise took place, and a pattern began to be set: bathes before breakfast, climbing the mast, points gained and lost during the day's sailing. The deck was covered with snow on the last night. Joe hailed Dr Alex Wood in a high wind near Thurne and praised God for the day he had encouraged him to study medicine at Cambridge. Joe also helped with an Easter camp for very poor boys from the slums of London's East End, and in August he and two of his sisters helped with the Whitby CSSM.

At the start of Joe's final year at Emmanuel he moved into a room in college. At about that time Florence sustained a serious accident when one of two guns belonging to the boys fell and went off as she was packing a school bag, wounding her seriously in the face. Bill, who had left it loaded, always felt himself responsible for this, and wrote in his memoir, 'Never shall I forget my mother's terrible scream as she fell to the ground . . . nor her forgiveness when next day she said, "I am so glad it happened to me, and not to you with life before you." ' But as Joe recalled, 'As we sat up with her most of the night a strange sense of anger came over me and I took the two guns outside and smashed them to bits against the wall of the house and threw the pieces into the shrubbery bushes.' Three days later it was decided to remove the damaged eye. Florence's remark was typical: 'You must come and watch the operation, Joe – it will be interesting for you.' As she slowly recovered, Florence approached her disability with the courage and practicality that characterized her whole life, and was soon back running everything again. And Joe commented, 'As a family this accident drew us all closer together. We were inclined to be too superficial and fond of teasing – this made us go deeper into the things of God and to be more open and honest with one another.'

In his last year, as well as starting a lifelong habit of swimming before breakfast all the year round, Joe continued to play with skill and energy in the Emmanuel College first XI hockey team: 'During my last winter at Cambridge we were unbeaten and we went to the top of the league. Written on my team photographs: 'Played 14, won 14; Lost 0. Score for 88, against 12.' He also became the college representative for the CICCU – a responsible task, which he tackled with his usual enthusiasm. And in February 1922, some students who had offered for the mission field set up the Cambridge University Missionary Band, who prayed for each other and kept in touch through newsletters for the rest of their lives. It was a splendid network of confident, dedicated, energetic young men who were to scatter to far-away countries – India, Africa, China, South America. Some would be bishops, some would work throughout their lives in relative obscurity serving remote communities. Later, Joe was to work closely with some of them abroad. Although he had no idea yet where God was calling him, his certainty of God's call was becoming stronger than ever. In June he took his degree and left the university. 'On my knees that night I thanked God for the way he had led me step by step and I dedicated my life afresh to him. My goal of becoming a doctor was in sight.'

4

The Family Tree

One day some years earlier, Joe's father had called him to
his study – the special room they rarely entered and around
which on Saturdays Florence made the children whisper,
because 'dear Dad was preparing his sermon'. From his
high bookshelves Edward produced a very old leather-
bound handwritten book. It was the record of the Church
family, beginning with a certain forbear named Samuel who
was boatswain on Charles II's royal yacht, 'Catherine',

about 1660, and his son Thomas, a shipwright at the time Peter the Great, Tsar of Russia, was instructed in shipbuilding on his incognito visit to Deptford in 1698. Turning the pages reverently Edward said, 'John, as eldest son you will have this one day, so keep it very carefully.'

The record is fascinating, and later Joe came to see close links between its story and his experiences in Africa. Samuel, the boatswain, is described as 'a man that had but little regard for religion', but the diary also records that 'it pleased the Lord to begin a work of grace in the heart of his son Thomas'. This came about through the influence of Thomas's second wife, Mary Newman, and led to the Church family's involvement for many years with a remarkable group of Christians called the Moravians.

The reformed and simple biblical teaching of John Wycliffe had inspired John Hus of Bohemia, and after Hus was burned at the stake in 1415, there remained groups of quiet seekers and thinkers living out his teaching. Such a group formed a society in 1457 called the *Unitas Fratrum* (Fellowship of the Brethren). Translating the Scriptures and circulating hymn books in the language of the people, they spread rapidly throughout Bohemia and neighbouring Moravia – the first of the Protestant churches. One of their leaders was Bishop Comenius, 'the father of modern education'. In 1620 at the start of the Thirty Years' War they were almost obliterated in the Battle of the White Mountain, and for a hundred years barely any trace of them remained. Then Count Zinzendorf began to give refuge to a few families who were fleeing from persecution in Moravia, on his estates at Herrnhut in Saxony. Among them were followers of Hus, Luther, Calvin and Zwingli, who, holding passionately to their particular beliefs, were 'somewhat disputatious'. This so distressed Zinzendorf that he visited every household and prayed with them, pleading with them to concentrate on the points on which they agreed. In May

1727 a Brotherly Agreement was drawn up in which they committed themselves to living together in love and unity. By August they felt ready to unite in a celebration of the Lord's Supper, and on 13 August 1727 in the course of the Holy Communion service the Holy Spirit fell upon the small gathered group in such power that the *Unitas Fratrum*, or the Moravian Church as it came to be called, was reborn with new life and vigour. The neat settlement at Herrnhut, with its chapel, school and quarters for the single brothers and the single sisters set the pattern, and with missionary zeal the revived church began to reach out to parts of the world where the Christian faith was not known.

In particular their gaze was directed to the new world of America, and they would sail up the Thames in London to wait at Greenwich and Deptford for ships heading for America and the West Indies. Here Mary and Thomas, the shipwright, who lived in Deptford, may first have come across them. The diary records that 'About the time of her husband's decease, which was in the year 1738, the Holy Ghost began to work upon Mary's heart in a more particular manner, by means of the Revd Whitefield and Wesley's preaching. She entered into the joy of the Lord, as she ceased to worry and found rest in the power of the Blood of Jesus.' John and Charles Wesley had themselves been converted to a living faith that same year, after John's friendship with the Moravian, Peter Bohler, and a subsequent visit to Herrnhut had convinced him that he lacked 'that faith whereby alone we are saved'. When Mary heard of the Brethren she said, 'This is the doctrine that will do for me, this I love and will abide by.' She was received into the congregation of the Moravians at Fetter Lane in 1749, and later into the Widows' Choir House. Joe Church recalled how two large oil paintings used to hang in the dining room at Cambridge looking down on them all: one a portrait of Mary, wearing the white bonnet and apron of the Moravian sisters with a large open Bible on her lap, the other probably her son Samuel. (Both portraits are unsigned, but are thought to be by the German artist Haidt who did portraits for the Moravians at Chelsea.)

Thomas and Mary's eldest son, Samuel, was apprenticed to a butcher in Deptford at the age of fourteen. Converted at a time of serious illness, he was clerk in the Dissenters congregation to which his father belonged, but 'when Mr Whitefield began to preach, I could have forsaken all to follow him'. On this account he was dismissed from the Dissenters and had to leave Deptford. His memoir records that 'He was exhibited at an ale-house in a painting over a chimney piece in the public tap-room, as standing under Mr Whitefield preaching on the mount at Blackheath, in his butcher's frock with "amen" attached to his mouth. This gave him no concern, but he rather rejoiced, esteeming it the reproach of Christ.' He was received into the Moravian congregation at Fetter Lane in 1748 and set up his own business at Spitalfields.

Samuel married Mary Bartlett, and their eldest son, John Christian, seceded from the United Brethren early in life and joined the established Church. A sugar refiner of Betts Street, Stepney, he died of a fit in his counting house aged forty-seven. William, the youngest son of John Christian and his wife, Sarah Elizabeth Hesse, was born in 1805 only 15 months before his father died. He continued in the family business of Church and Co., dried fruit and sugar importers, and it was he who compiled the family record. William's oldest brother John married Jane Couty, their son John Christian married Elizabeth Stubbs; Edward was their son, and Joe their grandson.

While some branches of the family concentrated on the business of importing and victualling, providing for the body, others of Thomas and Mary's descendants served God as missionaries and as ministers, feeding the soul. One of their daughters, Sarah, married John Syms, a butcher of Leadenhall Street who had sailed with George Whitefield as a missionary to America. It was during a missionary voyage to America in 1735 that Wesley, Whitefield and Ingham had first met the Moravians who influenced them so much, John Wesley noting their 'performing those servile offices for the other passengers which none of the English would undertake'. He noted too that when the sea poured over the deck, splitting the mainsail as the Moravians sang a psalm at the beginning of their service, 'A terrible screaming began among the English. The Germans calmly sang on.'

Thomas and Mary's youngest son, John, a Moravian brother, married Anna Chase, and two of their sons, John and Samuel Frederick, had remarkable and adventurous lives. *The Lebenslauf* – perhaps we would now call it a 'testimony' or spiritual journey – of John deserves publication in its entirety. It breathes a wonderful mixture of un-assuming Christian discipleship and high adventure. He was born in London in 1746. Because of his mother's ill-ness, he was brought up by the Brethren in Bedford from the age of five, where 'I thought that nothing should ever draw my heart aside from the object of its love, a dear cru-cified Saviour', but at seventeen, by now 'a slave to sinful inclinations', he returned to London to help his father in his business. His mother died in 1767, but not before she had begged the visiting Moravian Bishop Johannes to find places for him and his brother in one of the German con-gregations. On the way, at Zeist in Holland, in a wood at the back of the Single Brethren's garden, 'I poured out my soul before the Lord . . . He drew so inexpressibly near to my heart, that I was constrained to fall prostrate on the ground and give vent to my tears. I rose from the spot overcome with gratitude and, with a cheerfully resigned mind, committed my way unto the Lord.' Back in London and after further spiritual blessings and setbacks at Fetter

Lane, slowly and with much diffidence he began to feel that he was being called to serve God in some way in the congregation, and 'In the beginning of 1779 I quite unexpectedly received a call to be choir servant of the Single Brethren in Fulneck.' (The word 'choir' here denotes nothing to do with singing, but a 'group'. The Moravian congregations and settlements divided their members into such choirs – single brethren, single sisters, married couples, widows, girls, boys, etc.)

Fulneck was one of several Moravian settlements based on the Herrnhut model. The village was established in Yorkshire in 1746 on the initiative of Benjamin Ingham, a Church of England clergyman, friend of the Wesleys and member of the Fetter Lane Society, who had 'woken up to the fact that thousands of the people around him were as ignorant of the gospel as the Patagonians' and thought that the Brethren might bring them light. Over the next 17 years John Church ministered at Fulneck, at Gracehill in Northern Ireland, at Tytherton in Wiltshire and in Bath. In 1790, 'In Fulneck I entered into marriage with the Single Sister Elizabeth White, whom I took as from the hands of my dear Lord, and with whom, blessed be His name, I have lived in such heart's fellowship until this day.' Then in 1798 'I received a call to go to the island of Tobago, to have the direction of that Mission, and together with my wife, to assist in the labour among the negroes.'

This latest call was a shock to them both, but they were of one mind in praying and obtaining 'a willing mind to sacrifice every earthly consideration', and so, after many affectionate farewells from the brethren, they embarked from Portsmouth. Eventually, on 3 May, they sailed. In the Bay of Biscay 'the sea ran mountains high, awful and terrible to behold', but they were preserved, and arrived several weeks later first at Barbados, where John preached and 'baptized 4 negroes . . . with sensations I cannot describe', and then

Tobago. Here they ministered to the slave population for two years until John's poor health forced them to return to England. It was still some 30 years before the efforts of Wilberforce and others led to the abolition of the slave trade.

John's brother Samuel was trained as a cabinetmaker at the Brethren's house at Zeist in Holland. In 1786 he received a call to go out as a missionary to Jamaica, and 'in this view was married to the Single Sister Anna Rosina Hilger'. They were married at Herrnhut in 1786 and set out straightaway on a hazardous and uncomfortable journey by land and sea via Gravesend to Jamaica. Crossing the Atlantic they had no chairs or table, not even a cabin – only a piece of sailcloth fastened as a curtain to their bed. 'My wife, being the only female on board, and having no convenience suitable for her, was often brought into great straits.' There were other discomforts too: 'After we had been some time at sea, we perceived an intolerable stench about us, which daily increased. I began to search around, and discovered in a recess at the foot of our bed a bathing tub filled with turnips, carrots and parsnips in a high state of fermentation . . .' They eventually reached Jamaica, ending with a six-day journey round the island by canoe. 'After our arrival, many, and among the rest some medical gentlemen, expressed their assurance that we could not survive the fatigue, and exposure to drenching rain at night, and scorching sun by day, which we had undergone. But the Lord had determined otherwise.' They worked in Jamaica for five years and then returned to minister in several of the Moravian settlements in England.

Joe and his brothers and sisters loved to pore over this journal with its tales of the adventures of earlier members of the family. On the first page of the diary these words of the poet Cowper are inscribed:

> My boast is not that I deduce my birth
> From loins enthroned and rulers of the earth;
> But higher far my proud pretensions rise,
> The son of parents passed into the skies.

Near the Thames in London a large wooden door on a busy bend of Kings Road, Chelsea, opens into a quiet secret garden. Once part of the estate of Sir Thomas More, it is now the Moravian burial ground and here, under the modest gravestones of the brethren and sisters, interred separately in their 'choirs', some members of the Church family are buried. Joe Church commented as he meditated on the family journal:

> With the conversion of Thomas and Mary in the 18th century the whole complexion and character of the Church family tree changed . . . None can say exactly where revival begins. The stream runs in history on and on through the pages of time, though sometimes hidden. There is only one true beginning and that was at Calvary. 'Out of Him shall flow rivers of living water . . .' This is the true apostolic succession traced on through the lives of men and women. When a family or a member of it is linked with the invisible pipeline there begins to flow the water of life, through one member here and another there when he has come to the fountain to drink. So the East African Revival can be said to go back to John Wesley and the Moravians. But at this time of my story I understood none of these things.

5

1923–1927: Preparation

Joe describes in his own racy and inimitable way something of his time as a medical student at St Bartholomew's Hospital:

> Halfway down Pentonville Road, just before Kings Cross station, there used to be a lofty and grimy London vicarage standing back in its garden, called No. 1 Penton Place. After going down from Cambridge this became my home. Two widowed sisters kept on the family home after the last vicar, Stewart Dixon Stubbs (their father and my great-uncle), died, and ran it as a hostel for members and connections of the family studying medicine at the London hospitals. They had been in Pakhoi, China, for many years as CMS missionaries and the house was full of Chinese ornaments and bamboo bric-a-brac that rattled all day long as the trams ground their way up and down Pentonville Hill. We came to love 'No. 1 PP' and we soon learned all the short cuts on bikes to Bart's Hospital, ending by dodging frozen sides of beef in Smithfield Market before darting through the Henry the Eighth gateway to be in time for 9 o'clock lectures.

As always, sport took up a lot of time. In March 1923 Joe wrote in his diary, 'I find it very hard to keep fit in hospital. A doctor must keep himself fit.' He soon took steps to improve the situation. He became secretary of the first hockey XI and took care to arrange matches against excellent teams so that Bart's own standard improved. Partly because he was grateful to God for healing him earlier, and also because he sensed that physical and spiritual fitness were related, Joe took exercise seriously. He knew it was important to look after the body that God had given him. In this his father had set him a good example:

One of the earliest memories of our childhood days at Burrough Green was the sound of my father splashing in his early morning cold bath. The bath was a large circular one with handles and stood in the middle of my father's dressing room. Beside it there always used to stand a mysterious wooden box containing Tidman's sea salt. My father would emerge in his grey flannel nightgown from the bedroom where stood the large double bed in which we all were born, he would take a handful of 'Tidman's' and throw it into the bath, and the ritual began. There was much puffing and blowing and deep breathing and praise of the beneficent effects of 'Tidman's', then there would be a terrific drying 'to get the circulation going' and then a shout for the first one of the family to come . . . My father did not dragoon us and I think we were left to do much as we pleased, but we have grown up to enjoy cold baths and to find value, even spiritual value, in some of the Church family tough upbringing. I believe that physical fitness, runs before breakfast, riding in the early morning (my sisters used to ride the ponies), help to keep one nearer to God and alert mentally . . . Later on when we were 'on the house' and there was no time for games, we would change and run round the shiny deserted streets of London, sometimes after midnight. The dignified city police got to know those mad Bart's house surgeons as we rushed past, running down High Holborn and banking round opposite the Old Bailey, dodging the GPO mail vans as we entered the hospital Casualty Department entrance.

Spiritual exercise was important too, and most days at 1 o'clock, as at Cambridge, members of the Bart's Christian Union would meet in the little church of St Bartholomew's-the-less, the hospital's own ancient parish church, for a short time of prayer.

During this time, Joe took every opportunity of activity, adventure and service which came his way. In July 1923:

Putting into practice my theory that health was vital to doctors in training I decided to miss a three-months' appointment and entered instead on a 'once in a lifetime' experience, three weeks on a trawler in the North Sea. The idea came through a visit to Bart's of Sir Wilfred Grenfell who gave us an account of his work as a missionary doctor in Labrador. He said, 'If you want to come and help me in my work first go on a trial trip in the North Sea with the Mission to Deep Sea Fishermen and see how you like it.' He appealed to me greatly and I wondered if God was pointing me to serve him in Labrador or some such place.

A medical student on board would hold small clinics for fishermen of the North Sea fishing fleet. Although it did not eventually prove to be God's call, the experience proved fun and worthwhile. Joe continued his habit of daily swims by diving into the sea each morning. Many ideas for the Walrus cruises were picked up from the seamen on this trip,

including the Walrus theme song 'Windy Old Weather'. Other adventures that summer were the Whitby CSSM: 'a chance for the fourth time of learning the diagnosing and treating of the soul', and a Church Army weekend when he stood on a soapbox at Hyde Park Corner telling the story of how the Good Shepherd came to find him as he wandered the streets. Joe and two others also ran a Sunday evening gospel service at a mission called 'The Welcome' in a small street off Aldersgate.

In all these activities, Joe was preparing and training himself for whatever service God might eventually call him to. Even his sporting activities he saw as spiritual training:

> Games, riding or mountain climbing have a definite spiritual value later in life. In a good team you begin to know each other backwards, you trust each other, you learn unselfishness, you encourage each other, you 'put each other in the light'. If you don't pass the ball enough your mistakes can't be hidden . . . Many times I have used this picture to illustrate fellowship in action: 'Let the peace of God rule in your hearts' (Col. 3.15), where the Greek word for 'rule' can refer to a referee or umpire. In the game of life the Holy Spirit is the umpire, showing us instantly, if we will listen, what is not right and what is not 'the Highest'.

This idea of 'the Highest' was crucial in Joe's attitude to his Christian discipleship. So much so that he called his own autobiography *Quest for the Highest*. It was another way of describing the 'Victorious Life' already referred to: 'When we are fully surrendered to him (Jesus Christ), he fills our hearts with his presence and takes complete control, and wins all our victories for us. Such a life is a victorious life – a life of constant miracle.' (*How to Live the Victorious Life*, by an Unknown Christian). This life the unknown author also described as 'The Highest', and this was the way Joe sought to follow from his student days right through to old age.

The first official Walrus cruise took place in April 1924 under the flag of the CSSM, and in August, despite working for his finals day and night, Joe managed one week with the CSSM at Sheringham, 'a special time for the Church family because my brothers Bill and Howard came with me as workers, Bill from Emmanuel College, Cambridge, where he too was now studying medicine. This time was I think the sealing of God's call for them both for they later went also to Africa as missionaries, one to Ruanda and one to Kenya. My brother Howard was later to be greatly used during the Mau Mau rebellion.' There had also been a great gathering in Cambridge in July for the first Church family wedding, that of Joe's second sister Mary to his old school-friend, Rupert Penn, when a glorious summer wedding day was celebrated in punts on the 'backs'. Despite all these extra activities, Joe managed to pass his finals in five years instead of the usual six, claiming war service exemption.

'With the promise to serve God anywhere He should send me always in my mind and prayers, I was beginning to learn all I could about missionary societies and the countries where they worked. Every day I asked God to open up the way in his own time to my life's work for Him abroad.' More pressingly, he now faced an important decision as to where to do his house surgeon year. He decided in view of his calling to go abroad as a missionary that a provincial hospital would give him better experience; so he headed for Addenbrooke's Hospital, Cambridge where he started work as house surgeon and casualty officer at the end of October. Although he lived in the hospital, this was a coming home for Joe who knew Cambridge so well. He linked up with the Cambridge Inter-Collegiate Christian Union (CICCU) again, and particularly with its missionary branch, the Cambridge Volunteer Union. Almost immediately something of special significance occurred, when in November the speaker at a missionary breakfast was Dr Algie Stanley Smith, who told of a remarkable new opening for Christian medical work in the little-known country of Ruanda in the Belgian part of East Africa. To Joe the call to Africa seemed to come with unmistakeable clearness: 'All I could do was to say, "Here am I: send me".' At first it seemed that the Church Missionary Society (CMS) might not accept him for Ruanda because of lack of funds, but a special gift of £250 for two years from a friend of the Ruanda Mission met the need.

The 1926 Walrus cruise in April comprised six boats and 32 officers and older schoolboys. Bathes before breakfast, climbing the mast, sea shanties and laughter as well as careful mastering of the skills of sailing in all weather, and eventually the full days would end as they 'bowed in prayer before the One who loved to meet with fishermen and

young people beside the Sea of Galilee'. Later, as he travelled all over the world, Joe would meet one and another servant of God who owed his faith to those early Walrus cruises on the Broads.

Then, having completed his six months at Addenbrooke's, Joe went back to Bart's for a three-month speciality in dermatology. After that, 'I left London before my appointment ended for a weekend at Keswick, the first of many visits to that convention in the hills of England's Lake-land. The experience of the hymns sung with deep feeling from the depth of surrendered hearts in the vast tent, the friendship of young people, and older ones too, never left my memory.' Joe also described how 'In those days accepted missionary candidates of the CMS spent some time at the CMS summer school at Malvern in August before going to Foxbury or Liskeard Lodge for training. My experience there in the first week of August was memorable for me because of the beautiful summer and the fact that Decima Tracey, my future fiancée, was with us in the house party.'

This was not Joe's first meeting with Decima. Her brothers had been involved with Walrus cruises. Through this link, she was invited to live at 'No. 1 PP' as a medical student at the Royal Free Hospital. On the evening when Joe left Bart's to start his term as a house doctor at Addenbrooke's it was she who had helped him get ready. As his diary recorded: 'Packed with Decima till midnight.' And as Joe commented later, 'Another cryptic note in the form of a prayer shared only with God asked if perhaps she might be the one with whom I was to share my life.'

After the CMS Summer School, Joe spent three weeks leading the senior boys' houseparty at the Southwold CSSM on the Suffolk coast. He recalled:

We took part in all the CSSM activities and built vast sand pulpits on the beach, but the most memorable thing was the remarkable way that the Holy Spirit came down upon that little camp. I wrote at the time: 'The Lord truly walked in the midst of our camp'. It was a time of consecration and reconsecration of life to Him. All the boys who were there at the end had definitely decided for Christ and some wanted to be missionaries abroad later on. Amongst those who took Christ as their Saviour were Roy and Brian Hession who were the moving spirits of the party . . . little did we know that those days at Southwold would lead Roy and me to travel together many thousands of miles round the world in later years, preaching the gospel and holding convention meetings calling people to hear the challenge of revival.

Then followed five months in Belgium to learn French and to take the Diploma of Tropical Medicine and Hygiene. From here he wrote in a prophetic letter to *Ruanda Notes*, 'God has given us a glorious opening in Ruanda. Please pray that this part of Africa may be a great centre for evangelism and revival.' And, ever practical as well as spiritual, he added, looking ahead to the Walrus cruises that April: 'I had a great brainwave the other day. I thought that we might be able to show Dr Smith's Ruanda slides on the mainsail of one of the yachts at night . . .' Whether they did, history doesn't relate.

Back in England came two consecutive weeks of Walrus cruises in April 1927, with 52 boys booked in for each. Joe was working hard for the second part of the Cambridge degree of MB, B Chir which he had to take in June. He was speaking about Ruanda as much as he could at weekend meetings, travelling around the country on a newly acquired Model P Triumph motor bicycle with a sidecar. He was also courting his future bride. A week before his exam, Joe took Decie to stay with his family in Cambridge, and on a beautiful June day they went out to a part of the Fens beyond Fen Ditton to a family picnic spot at the end of a long lane leading down to the Cam. 'We walked up and down that lane I don't know how many times and at last I sprung the great question. From that moment we belonged to each other "for better, for worse, till death do us part".'

Decima was the tenth child in a large and interesting family who lived at Willand in Devon. Her father was a family doctor. One of her brothers, Hugh, emigrated to South Africa where he became an expert in African traditional music and established the International Library of African Music; another brother, Christopher, was later to be Acting Governor of the Sudan. All intellectual and clever, they came to like and respect Joe, so that another of Decie's brothers, Basil, wrote in his diary after an afternoon together at the Varsity hockey match (when Joe's brother Bill was playing for Cambridge), 'I have enjoyed this afternoon immensely. I always feel this in Joe's presence; I put it down to his religion, and love it and him the more.'

Decima had brown hair and dark-brown eyes and was quiet, thorough, reliable and kind. She was very musical, singing and playing various instruments. Most important to Joe, she was a committed Christian dedicated to 'the Highest' like himself. Joe wrote to his old friend and brother-in-law, Rupert Penn:

The Lord has just been too marvellous. What more can a man want than the Lord Jesus and an out-and-out girl who loves him! We went up the backs in a punt one glorious night after the John's concert while the Trinity Ball was on, and we stayed out until 3 o'clock – disgraceful! Mother and Pater didn't mind – we had so little time to be together. Decima has lived at PP for 2 years and helped me with missions a lot and is just out and out now for the Lord. She knows me and my failings and my hobbies and we have everything in common. She's jolly musical and can play anything. She hopes to be qualified in 18 months and I expect we shall get married out in Ruanda – those 18 months, what a horrid thought!

Decie's mother insisted that she complete her qualifications. She came top of her final year for surgery, but did no house jobs. And as Joe commented ruefully, 'I won my help-meet for life but I failed my MB and never found time to sit for it again. I took the London MRCS, LRCP to save time.' Then, after an operation to remove a damaged knee cartilage and a 'grand safari' visiting 14 CSSM beach missions around the coast of England on his motorbike to elicit prayer support for the work in Ruanda, he finally began to prepare to leave. The Officers' Christian Union had presented the Ruanda Mission with an 18 ft motor sailing boat called *The King's Own* for use in Africa. Joe went to Littlehampton for a short launching ceremony to dedicate it to God before it was dismantled and packed in sections for shipping. The last few weeks' journeys between London and Cambridge, buying a tent, tropical kit, safari outfit and rifle, taking his Triumph to be crated and sent to the ship, and fitting in goodbye meetings, allowed valued time for reflection. The CICCU invited him to a farewell tea at the Dorothy café in Cambridge when they announced that Joe was to become their 'own missionary', a privilege he was to hold for 37 years. This meant, of course, that they prayed for him and for his work throughout that time.

Particularly through the book already mentioned, *How to Live the Victorious Life*, there was a strong expectation within the CICCU of revival – of a movement of God's Spirit which would breathe new life and vigour into the church and its outreach, much as the revivals involving the Moravians and then the Wesleys and Whitefield had done in the eighteenth century. Many years later Joe wrote this: 'How much did the revival movement that came to Ruanda and the churches of East Africa owe to the CICCU daily

prayer meetings in the Henry Martyn Hall? Who can ever
know?' Only a few years before, Dr Algie Stanley Smith had
written, while working in Western Uganda, 'A safari round
the village churches always sends one to one's knees in
prayer for a revival of spiritual religion.' So after a rousing
send-off from Ruanda supporters and Broads campers at
Liverpool Street station in London, Joe set sail for Africa
from Tilbury on 28 October 1927, inspired with that vision
of revival.

Decie and he knew that they would not see each other
again for two-and-a-half years. The ship's siren sounded,
the gangways were removed and the waving figures grew
smaller and smaller as the *Modasa* crept out of Tilbury
docks and turned into the Thames estuary; and England
was soon blotted out in the October fog.

6

1857–1925: Background

The opening in Ruanda was indeed remarkable, and its story went back some years. Seventy years earlier, in December 1857, David Livingstone had made his famous appeal to students in a speech at the Senate House in Cambridge: 'I beg to direct your attention to Africa. I know that in a few years I shall be cut off in that country which is now open; do not let it be shut again! I go back to Africa to try to make an open path for commerce and Christianity. Do you carry out the work which I have begun; I leave it with you.' His concern was for the spreading of the good news of Jesus Christ, and for a healing of 'the open sore of the world' – the elimination of the African slave trade. The explorations of Burton, Speke, Grant, Baker, Livingstone and Stanley opened the path, but they also made possible the 'scramble for Africa', formalized at a conference in Berlin in 1884 with no reference to the African people themselves, in which commercial interests led to the taking over of parts of the country by different European powers, Britain notable among them with her hope of an all-British corridor south to north linked by a Cape-to-Cairo railway.

The immediate spiritual response to Livingstone's challenge was that of the ill-fated Universities Mission to Central Africa, most of whose pioneers met their deaths soon after setting off up the Zambesi. Then in 1875, a few years after his famous meeting with Livingstone, the explorer Stanley reached Uganda and, encouraged by the response of Mutesa, King of the Baganda, wrote a letter to the *Daily Telegraph* in London, echoing in Mutesa's name Livingstone's appeal for missionaries. The response was prompt, and the first members of the Church Missionary Society reached Zanzibar in June 1876 and moved on to Uganda. The next 20 years saw much tragedy and confusion as Protestants and Roman Catholics, frustrated not only by each other but by the brutality of Mutesa's son, the new King Mwanga, were sucked into an escalating civil war. Many, some not much more than children, were killed for their faith. According to Bishop Stephen Neill, 'the exact number of martyrs is not known; all witnesses bear testimony to the courage and serenity with which they met their death' (*A History of Christian Missions. The Pelican History of the Church*, IV, p. 386). In 1885 the Anglican Bishop Hannington was speared to death by the orders of Mwanga. Eventually, in 1894, the efforts of Captain Lugard led to the establishment of the British Protectorate, the country was divided into spheres of Protestant and Roman Catholic influence, and peace and order were restored.

The Bible had been translated by two other Uganda pioneers, Mackay and Pilkington. As Ugandan Christians carried the gospel from village to village, the blood of the martyrs proved indeed to be the seed of the church, as the church was swept by revival and grew rapidly. To quote Stephen Neill again, 'Converts began to come in, in hundreds and then in thousands . . . Nothing is more remarkable in the early history of the Uganda Church than the evangelistic zeal with which its Christians were inspired.'

A great cathedral was built on Namirembe Hill above Kampala; on the slopes of the hill too, Mengo Hospital was founded in 1897 by Dr Albert Cook. It was Dr Cook, visiting England looking for recruits for the hospital, who invited two young medical students, Algie Stanley Smith and Leonard Sharp, both graduates of Cambridge and now doing their hospital training in London, to help him in Mengo Hospital. They arranged to sail in October 1914. In the event, with the outbreak of war Mengo became a base military hospital for the Uganda section of the East African forces, and both doctors were drafted there to help Dr Cook.

But from their student days at Cambridge they had longed to take the gospel where it had not been heard before. They were convinced that Uganda was a starting point for something else, and they were waiting for God to show them what it was. In 1916 their interest was drawn to a book, *The Heart of Africa*, by the Duke of Mecklenberg, which described the twin kingdoms of Ruanda-Urundi, then part of German East Africa, to the south of Uganda. The account of this remote highland country, much of it a mile above sea level, cool and beautiful, began to fill the young men's minds. They read of the people, the indigenous population, the agricultural Bahutu, dominated by the tall and aristocratic Batutsi, cattle owners and athletes, descendants of tribes thought to have migrated from North Africa, and a third minority element, groups of pygmies (huntsmen and potters). As the Allied forces drove the Germans out of their East African territories, descriptions of Ruanda began to reach the base hospital at Mengo, and the doctors' interest grew steadily deeper. In December 1916, they applied to the Ugandan Government for permission to spend their local leave touring Ruanda, and by a curious mistake in which God's hand seemed to overrule the rules of men, the necessary permits were given. The Belgian troops occupying Ruanda should have been consulted but were not. Happily oblivious, the two doctors set off.

They travelled by motorbike from Kampala to the

border, then trekked by foot for three more days, finally climbing the last steep escarpment to look down for the first time into Ruanda. As they gazed down at the green hills glowing in the evening light and the drifts of smoke from myriads of huts, both were convinced that this was where God was calling them to work. They toured northern Ruanda for nearly three weeks, discovering a beautiful country that lies on the upland of the chain of mountains which form the backbone of Africa and the watershed of the Congo and the Nile. To the north-west are the Bufumbira mountains, eight volcanoes standing out like sentinels

against the sky on a clear evening; to the west the Great Rift Valley which divides Rwanda and Burundi from Zaire; to the east, the dry plains of Tanzania.

By 1919, their commission in Uganda completed, the war was over and Ruanda-Urundi, like neighbouring Congo, was under Belgian mandate. The two doctors went back to England and somehow persuaded the already overstretched Church Missionary Society that, subject to the consent of the Belgian authorities, and if the doctors could raise the funds for the new work, they should extend their work into Ruanda-Urundi. At first it seemed that they had been given the necessary consent from the Belgian Government to work alongside Belgian

Protestants in Urundi, but then, when they had already started on their journey out, this was withdrawn. By February 1921 Algie and Leonard and their young wives, Zoë (Leonard's sister) and Esther, had arrived in Uganda, and as they could not work in Ruanda itself they were sent to a neighbouring part of Uganda called Kigezi, a wild, mountainous region near to the Bufumbira range, to be based a mile from the small Government post of Kabale. In no time, and with the help of enthusiastic local Christians, the mud and wattle huts of a hospital began to go up. The work grew rapidly, and three years later Leonard Sharp went back to England and recruited more people to join the team: Captain Geoffrey Holmes, ex-army and very much a pioneer; the Rev Jack Warren, teacher and pastor; Miss Margaret Davis, a pharmacist; and in 1925 the Rev Harold Guillebaud, to work on Bible translation with his wife.

Soon, as well as the hospital, there was a girls' school, a boys' school and a big church at Kabale. But all was far from well in the burgeoning Christian community and, although African teachers and evangelists were going long distances taking the gospel throughout Kigezi and beyond, the spiritual quality of many of their lives was deeply disappointing, so much so that in 1927 Jack Warren wrote asking for special prayer: 'There are now close on two thousand baptized Christians, but we are only too conscious that the signs of real heart-change are very few and far between. Moral lapse upon lapse, and tragedy upon tragedy, have been following one on top of the other. Only this week comes the evidence that one of our most trusted teachers has been stealing the church members' money. Another senior teacher has been drinking heavily and has been dismissed. We plead with every Friend of Ruanda to set aside a time on each of ten days to wrestle in prayer with us, and then we know that we may indeed expect a wonderful outpouring of the Holy Spirit, not limited to Kigezi, but a flood that will reach to the uttermost parts of Ruanda in days to come.'

While all this was happening in Kigezi in Uganda, progress was also being made in Ruanda itself. As far back as 1922, the Sharps and Stanley Smiths at Kabale were thrilled to learn that the Belgian Government had agreed to transfer a wide strip of Eastern Ruanda to Britain for the purpose of surveying the Cape-to-Cairo railway. They met the District Commissioner of 'British Bufumbira' and it seemed that God was answering their prayers and opening the door for which they had been waiting since their reconnaissance of 1916. They were given complete freedom to travel around and to choose a place to begin work. Wherever they went, crowds gathered for medical treatment and people asked for teachers. Initially they had no spare missionaries, but the Church of Uganda responded by sending dedicated pastors, like the Rev Seniei Muganda Wasula, ordained at Bishop Tucker Memorial College, Mukono, who found living in Ruanda hard. As he wrote: 'These are the things I have seen here: hills, and nothing but hills stretching everywhere; bitter cold exceeding that of Uganda; the food consisting of two kinds of flour, peas, beans and a few potatoes, but this food gives us no joy. However, we look not at the earthly joy, for ours is a heavenly joy in Christ Jesus.'

By 1924 the strip of British territory was handed back to Belgium. The British withdrew and the railway project was abandoned but, miraculously, agreement was obtained for the continuing work of the CMS's Ruanda Mission on what was now foreign soil. Once again God had overruled the muddles made by man. From Kabale, the small mission sent Geoffrey Holmes, vigorous and athletic (he had been Captain of the British Army Ice Hockey Team), to make links with the local people and to choose a site. He went with his motorbike and tent and was soon on terms of friendship with the Tutsi King Musinga and his chiefs at the Royal Court at Nyanza: 'a race of gentlemen with beautiful physique, undoubtedly as fine as the world produces, keen on games and sport,' he found them, 'but proud, arrogant and cruel.' The site he chose was Gahini hill, at the east end of Lake Mohasi and at the junction of two important travel routes. Soon two others joined him to form a small team: the Rev Herbert Jackson and Kosiya Shalita.

Kosiya's story was extraordinary. Son of a local high chief, his family, following an uprising some 30 years earlier, had fled from the Gahini district to Uganda, where under God's hand he became a Christian and received an excellent education. He was a student at King's College, Budo, when Dr Stanley Smith appealed for people to go as missionaries to Ruanda; and who better suited than Kosiya, to go back to his own people and birthplace? As he himself wrote, 'Who knew that I was going to work to tell my own people near where I was born about God, when I did not know him myself when I left the place? God knew. He took me out of my own country for that purpose. He took me out for *good* which my people called *danger*.'

With their official position still insecure, based only on the sanction of individual Administrators rather than on Belgian Government approval, the small team worked hard, teaching, preaching, dispensing simple medicines from Gahini and other centres nearby. They even began to build a hospital. But more resources were needed, and in 1925 Dr Stanley Smith visited England both to arrange the setting up of the Ruanda General and Medical Mission as an independent auxiliary of the CMS, and to ask for new recruits. It was then that he visited Cambridge and Joe Church heard God's call. Joe was the one whom God had been preparing to come as the doctor to Gahini hospital.

7

1927–1928: To Gahini

Mombasa, Nairobi, Kampala. From there a 280-mile journey by motorbike along the rough road to Kabale where Joe arrived on the evening of 20 December, 'sore and blistered, to see Leonard Sharp in his Trinity College Cambridge blazer on the road with the Kabale schoolboys all lined up to greet me. My long journey to the centre of Africa was ended. I settled down to live in a little thatched single roomed hut near the Sharps' house, which became my home for six months while I learned the ropes of mission work and began regular language study.'

He watched the other missionaries at work: Len Sharp, operating with meticulous care, or using his skilled hands to draw plans of a church or a school building, and exercising equal precision in the sport of big game hunting (once he ducked as an angry lion charged him and calmly shot it through the mouth as it jumped over his head). Len gave Joe an Airedale puppy which he loved and trained to sit on the tank of his motorbike, but to Africans all dogs were untouchable, you did not pat them or let them lick you, so Joe learnt to be sensitive to their feelings . . . Then there was Algie Stanley Smith with his gift of always being there when you were in trouble and needed him most, a careful listener and counsellor; Harold Guillebaud, surrounded by grammars and concordances, deep in translation – or reading to his family from some amusing book propped up in front of him at meals, apparently oblivious to his food; and Jack Warren, MC of World War I, stricken with TB, teaching the elements of drilling and self-discipline to the Kigezi schoolboys.

Almost at once Joe learnt of difficulties between hospital and church: the 'three-legged stool' of the work of the CMS – church, schools, hospital – was in danger of becoming unbalanced. And watching the huge crowds in their damp goatskins who had walked since dawn through the mist to join in the Christmas service, he realized something of the dangers of a mass movement in which a population group might turn to Christianity without coming personally to the cross in repentance and faith. In January Joe paid a brief visit with Geoffrey Holmes to the place where his life's work was to be: Gahini hill, rising up out of the blue waters of Lake Mohasi in Ruanda. He was appalled by the poverty and sickness of the people, but couldn't stay then, heading instead straight back to Kabale for a special week of prayer and Bible study, as a result of which 20 Ugandan evangelists and eight hospital workers offered to serve God in Ruanda. Joe's enthusiasm for Ruanda soon caused trouble with two fellow missionaries who, seeing a map he had taken round England announcing 'Christ died for Ruanda', accused him of belittling the work they had been doing in Kigezi. In their opinion the CMS should never have started work in Belgian territory. Already, after only a few weeks in Africa, Joe was uncovering sore spots and 'molehills which were becoming mountains'.

In April Joe went with Algie on his first foot safari to village churches:

We crossed Lake Bunyoni ('place of the birds') in the early morning in narrow canoes hewn out of tree trunks, and then spent hours foot-slogging up into the bamboo forest, often

travelling along elephant tracks, till we suddenly came out onto an escarpment. Near the top, Algie said to me, 'Joe, you are going to see one of the most wonderful views in the world.' We had come out near the famous Kanaba gap, now a tourist attraction. It was as though part of the surface of the moon had become covered with tropical vegetation two thousand feet below us. The whole vast valley was pitted with extinct volcanoes while in the background towering up into the clouds was the line of the Bufumbira volcanoes. Thousands of healthy Africans live in this fantastically fertile plain where giant vegetables grow in the volcanic soil.

Next day they reached Kisoro in the valley, to be greeted by the Christians lined up along the road. There were to be baptisms at Easter, and now Algie sat for hours helping the

senior catechist question the candidates. It was apostolic
work and Joe was thrilled to be involved. The sight of the
huge mountain Muhavura towering over the Kisoro plain
at just under 14,000 feet was a challenge too, and shortly afterwards he went up it and down again in one day – the first
person to achieve this, as far as he knew. On another occasion he and Bert Jackson climbed another of the range –
Sabinio, which no African would tackle as it had a taboo on
it. Having reached the summit – the first people to do so –
they started climbing down again in thick mist, only to realize just in time that they had gone over the lip of the preci-
pice inside the crater and were in moments of dropping to
their deaths.

A few weeks later Joe joined Len on a medical safari to
the game country around Lake Edward – now the Queen
Elizabeth National Park – where sleeping sickness was rife.
As he commented:

> In those days it was almost like visiting another world, a pre-
> historic world of salt lakes and big game running wild, undis-
> turbed by human beings. It was more than a 'sportsman's
> paradise' for me, because I saw in it a glimpse of an unspoilt
> world that has remained with me all my life . . . The next few
> days were spent in examining patients for sleeping sickness at
> the few fishing villages, hunting to provide for the porters and
> collecting a few trophies for the walls of my room. We still
> mounted the horns in those days. As Len and I stalked the buf-
> falo together and faced the danger of their cunning, I think we
> found depths of oneness in Christ that were very profound. We
> did not always see eye to eye in the methods of big game hunt-
> ing or in the problems of revival later on, but these times of
> hunting and danger bound us together in a very deep way.

In one of several adventures they shared, Len and Joe
wounded a huge elephant, and then, in honour bound to

finish it off, tracked it uphill. Suddenly it saw them, and thundered down towards them like an express train. As the two men separated, it veered towards Len, and Joe quickly swung behind a tree and shot it broadside on. Len was knocked down by its front feet and landed in its track but mercifully with its feet to either side of him. The elephant collapsed and died, and Len's rifle was later found 40 feet away.

Once his medical work was done, Joe loved to go trophy hunting, pitting his wits against the strength of the huge East African wild animals. He was not only 'holy Joe, the missionary', he was also Joe the sportsman, keen to make it into the record books. With his shooting skills which went back to his early days at Burrough Green, these opportunities were wonderful for Joe, and all part of the big adventure which, together with his clear sense of God's call, had drawn him to Africa. But although big game hunting was then still very much accepted, there were those back at the mission base at Kabale who were not so sure. Joe continues:

I brushed aside one or two criticisms – that hunting was too dangerous and was it really necessary? I loved every minute of it, especially when I was with someone whom I looked up to immensely as a man of God like Leonard Sharp. But God brought a challenge to me through the Irish forthrightness of Constance Hornby, a senior missionary, who had leanings towards anti-vivisection and was against hunting of any kind. I had been called out by a Muchiga [a local tribe in Kigezi] neighbour who lived near the mission station to help him deal with a leopard that was killing his goats. I carefully learned how to make a two-partitioned trap with logs, one part with a live goat safely inside it, and the front part with a shotgun and tripwire which would get the intruder first. But it was the thought of the night of fear for the small goat that Miss Hornby tried to get me to see. In the argument that followed she overstated her case saying, 'I don't mind what happens to you but it's bringing suffering to the animals . . .' This remark stuck in my mind and comes into the story later, when I was carried into Kabale having been badly mauled by a leopard.

Soon Joe's five months at Kabale were at an end:

I had learnt enough Lunyaruanda (the language of Ruanda) to preach a very halting sermon. Everyone had been extremely kind and had put up with my endless questions and new ideas and many shortcomings. ['I thought him a very immature young man,' said an older missionary. 'He always seemed to be chasing butterflies.'] Life had been full and enjoyable. On 2 June 1928, the lorry left before dawn, piled high with my *bintu* (belongings) on top of which was my portable bamboo and canvas boat, my house boy Muterahejuru, called 'Mut', my Airedale puppy and my monkey, named 'Cuss', bequeathed to me by the Sharps. I followed on my *piki piki*, an onomatopoeic word for motorbike, to pick up the bits on the 100-mile journey to Gahini, my future home.

Joe's account of his arrival at Gahini merits quoting almost in full:

There was no customs post at the frontier between the British and Belgian territories in those days, not even a tree trunk across the road. There was a gentlemen's agreement to report to the Belgian *Administrateur Territorial* at Gatsibu, 35 miles further on. It was the beginning of the long dry season, the air was heavy with the scent of flowering acacia trees, and the foot-tracks and the newly traced-out motor road were lined with yellow wild sunflowers. From Gatsibu I went ahead of the lorry, there was no holding the *piki* back! But I had gone only a few miles when I spotted an incredible cavalcade coming slowly towards me in the distance. It consisted of about nine Africans on loaded-up bicycles led by a man wearing a pith helmet on a motorbike, going very slowly with a white bundle suspended from the handle bars. I waved and drew alongside, and Geoffrey Holmes flopped over onto the grass bank beside the road and proceeded to undo a heavily bandaged leg which was unloosed from the front of the bike. I was greeted with 'Hullo, Joe, old boy. Welcome to Gahini!' He brushed off the flies as he got down nearer to a large discharging tropical ulcer above the ankle. 'But Geoff' I said, 'You must put that leg up and rest it.' His answer was typical: 'I'm all right, old man. I'm going up to Gatsibu. I don't want to be a bother to you.' As I watched this extraordinary group move off slowly until it disappeared into the distance, I was deeply moved at my fellow missionary's not wanting to bother me with his foul tropical ulcer. (He took my advice and strung his leg to the ridge pole of his tent. During the night, thus immobilized, he was visited by thieves and all his belongings were taken.) I discovered later that Geoff had another reason for leaving Gahini: he wanted to give me a free hand there, and yet it was he who had explored it first and obtained the concession for the Mission on the smooth grassy hill at the east end of the lake. His passion was to press on with the pioneering of the gospel. He also wanted me to have his room in the single house we were all occupying.

Covered in dust and burnt by the sun I rounded the last bend of Lake Mohasi as the setting sun lit up the dry hillside of Gahini facing westwards over the 30-mile-long lake. Was this really to be my home and the scene of my life work, I thought? The men laboriously making the road round the lake were resting on their worn-out hoes. As I greeted them, '*Muraho, mwese!*' they surveyed this strange new *muzungu* (white man) but their expressions seemed to say, 'Oh here is just one more *muzungu* who has come to make us work!' Why had I come to this deserted spot, I thought? What had I come to do in this barren place? I remember a great depression coming over me, an anti-climax, as I revved up the overheated engine and roared up the very steep hill.

Joe, Bert Jackson and Kosiya Shalita talked over supper about this country of such contradictions – superb beauty and yet abject poverty; a healthy climate and yet staggering malnutrition and so much disease: everywhere men, women and children with the ulcers, scarring and deformities of yaws. As they talked, Joe saw very clearly that 'God had put Gahini in the centre of a quarter of a million people without medical aid and without the gospel of the love of God. I knew now why I had come. I never doubted it again.' And he would not have to carry the medical burden alone: 'During the night of my stop at Gatsibu for customs formalities God had spoken very clearly about a second doctor for Gahini. I had almost heard the voice say, "Write to your brother Bill and ask him to come to join you." Bill had just written to say he had heard the call to the mission field. I knew my brother's thoroughness and ability to stick at things in difficult situations and I felt I needed him. That was a call from God that resulted in our working for many years together.'

But for the moment Joe was plunged without Bill's help into a deepening crisis. The rains had failed for two seasons and the long dry season was beginning. Already there was a serious shortage of food. Rough grass shelters were packed with thin apathetic people sitting over the embers of their fires or lying on the ground sick and exhausted. Joe began work straightaway, carrying out his first operation on a chief who had been carried 30 miles with huge multiple abscesses; distributing such food as was available; organizing those who were strong enough to start again to build a hospital with sun-dried bricks – work which had ceased because of the famine – and paying them where possible with food; seeing outpatients in the grass 'wigwams' which served as a temporary hospital. Two different treatments had recently been discovered for yaws, and as these medicines were brought from Kampala and injected, the name of Gahini spread and more and more people came.

Joe enjoyed planning the new hospital, and clearly had a gift for it. He described how, having begun by making the bricks, 'the walls of the hospital began to rise out of the grass, the window frames went in and, just at the right time, a load of roof timber, black wattles grown with Len's forethought at Kabale, brought by lorry, ground its way up the steep road we had just finished to the hospital. Likewise mysteriously a load of galvanized iron appeared. Neither Kosiya nor I knew much about building, but all this activity did us good. It took our minds off the horror of famine and suffering that daily hung over us. We felt better to be doing something.'

In fact, Joe was none too well himself. He had had two falls on his motorbike on his journey to Gahini and these had led to ulcers which were getting worse, one on his ankle and the other on his knee. He treated himself as best he could, but they made him feel generally run down. He tried to rest but there was too much to be done. As he described:

My letters to my mother and my fiancée were full of *joie de vivre* but there was a sense of increasing difficulties. Post was difficult. It took at least two months to get an answer to letters from England as there was no airmail then. The remembered comfort and ease of life at Kabale stood out in contrast to what seemed to us a fight for life at Gahini. I think we used to be nagged by the feeling that we were not so efficient as those at Kabale. The ants were worse. Our buildings fell down. Our friends were afraid to come and stay at Gahini which became known as a death trap for disease – jiggers, the burrowing fleas which can cripple and even prove fatal, reached plague proportions. And God allowed me to have another testing. I was operating on a case of probable syphilis and pricked my finger.

I removed my gloves and injected antiseptic into the spot but I could not get rid of worry, till it came to me that God wanted me to repent more deeply of wrong thoughts and this was his warning. So it was a new surrender and time of praise again. Now I see that God was allowing these testings for a special purpose.

The new volunteers had arrived from Kabale. With the floors of two rooms of the hospital now bricked, one day towards the end of June they helped Joe move the first 15 patients from the 'wigwams', and that evening, by moonlight, Joe did his first ward round with Paulo Gahundi, a volunteer hospital dresser, amid the ghostly walls of unroofed rooms. Joe, Kosiya and his hospital staff began to have prayers in Joe's bedroom every day after breakfast, and at the same time Joe began preaching to the outpatients: 'I found a crowd of outpatients waiting. I took a stool out and put it on an anthill, and with Paulo beside me, the Batutsi on one side and the Bahutu on the other, we explained to them that we were going to pray to God to help us by his Holy Spirit to be healed in our bodies and in our hearts. Then I told them impromptu how God had sent his Son, Jesus, into the world to heal us and save us, and that was why we were there.'

What a curious situation this was – Joe himself looked like a representative of the colonial power, but was Protestant and English, not Roman Catholic and Belgian. His African Christian leaders from Uganda spoke neither Lunyaruanda nor French. And the people of Gahini, although they did all speak one language, were of two different races or classes: the Tutsi, the minority ruling class who had wealth (in the form of cattle) and education, and the Hutus who had neither, just their smallholdings on the land which was left from Tutsi grazing land. The Belgian Government and the Roman Catholic Church at this time favoured the Tutsis, running schools especially for the sons of chiefs. The Ruanda Mission, child of its time and looking for intelligent response and leadership, while aiming to be non-discriminatory and opening its hospital doors to all, tended inevitably to do the same.

There was a lot to do and, although his ulcers were healing, Joe was often exhausted: 'Sometimes at bedtime I would try to write to Decie but the line would just end in a blur . . . I would fall asleep out of sheer exhaustion; but it was a pleasurable exhaustion like the feeling one gets at the end of a match that you have really enjoyed. Sometimes I would just talk rubbish to my Airedale puppy that slept in my bedroom!' Sadly, Joe was soon to lose this good friend – the dog was accidentally shot on a night-time expedition to scare local hyenas. As Joe commented, 'I was staggered. I don't think I had ever felt bereavement so acutely before. He used to shadow me all day and lie at my feet for hospital prayers. Bert and I mused on it as we walked home and gave it to the Lord.'

A Belgian woman, Mrs Monti, who had been awaiting the arrival of her baby with her husband at Gahini and also doing some housekeeping for Joe and Bert, left in July with the baby, so Algie and Zoë Stanley Smith came from Kabale with their small children to help. Joe remembered:

We spotted the black speck of their car creeping slowly round the first bend of the lakeside road and then the drums were beaten for everyone to run out and give them a Gahini welcome. (Later we used to tell people to flash their headlights three times so that we could get food and baths ready for them.) Bert and Kosiya lined the people up along the road while I went down on the *piki* to escort them in, with their lorry following close behind. We gave them a room in the house and I moved into a tent for the time being. No rain had fallen over the two months since I had arrived, and everything was dry and dusty. The famine was getting worse.

8

1928–1929: Famine

In August 1928 Joe, Algie and Geoffrey Holmes set off along the lake in the motor boat for Kigali, the capital of Ruanda, to see the Belgian Resident. They obtained permission for the 15 new church teachers from Kabale to work in Ruanda, and Joe was given official recognition to practise medicine and to run dispensaries, two of which, at Gatsibu and Rukira, had already been started by Bert Jackson and Christians from Uganda. Walking back to the lake rejoicing, they were overtaken by an African shouting that a lion had taken a man from his bed and had killed and was eating him. Following, they found a crowd of Africans armed with sticks, spears, and bows and arrows looking down from a safe distance at a clump of elephant grass where the lion was resting after his feast.

The three sprang into action, taking up positions with their rifles. At a given signal, stones were thrown where the lion was, and a deep growling and snarling ensued. Then with a thrashing of the long grass, the lion's head appeared and with a roar it sprang twice into the air between Algie and Joe. Both rifles rang out at the same moment and the lion fell dead. As Joe commented, 'It was incredibly exciting. The Africans went mad with delight and began to do the famous lion dance as they rushed down the sides of the valley to where the lion was. One shot had gone through its head into the brain and the other was in its side. Pieces of the dead man's body were found in its stomach. We were late getting back and a storm blew up on the lake, but we felt God had been with us in helping those poor people who were being terrified by a lion turned man-eater.' They were able to provide such effective help because at that time they were the only people with guns. On another occasion the outcome was less happy:

One Sunday afternoon in October a man came running to our house to say they had seen a leopard hiding on the other side of the village and would I come quickly to help. I didn't normally hunt on Sundays but felt it was my duty to go. Kosiya and I went on the *piki* and were soon at the spot. Groups of frightened Africans were watching and pointing. I thought the leopard would almost certainly break cover and go down into the valley and we could shoot it as it ran. I gave Kosiya my shotgun and took the rifle. We advanced across open ground and threw two stones. Suddenly out came the snarling animal heading straight for us. Its ears were back and its claws were bared. It was coming at tremendous speed. I fired, but my first shot missed. I fired again and hit him at about 15 yards and he rolled over in a cloud of dust right on top of me, squashing me into the ground. I was conscious of the leopard's tremendous weight; it was shaking me and I remember praying. Its claws were in my back, thighs and right hand and shoulder, and it had bitten me right down to the bone across the top of my head. There was a lot of bleeding from my scalp-wounds which prevented me from seeing properly, and I heard Kosiya shouting for me to shoot.

Kosiya had pulled the leopard off Joe so that he could shoot again. And as Joe explained, 'Kosiya's bravery in staying with me turned its attention from me and it wanted to go for him, but it was mortally wounded and began to crawl away.

Then it paused and looked round as though it was coming back. I fired once more and it was all over.' Many years later, and shortly before his death, Kosiya told the story from his point of view to Joe Church's sons who were visiting Uganda. He described his dilemma: he and Joe alone miles out in the bush, Joe severely wounded, and no way to reach help apart from the motorbike which Kosiya had never driven. He did the only thing possible – got Joe, bleeding and weak, onto the machine with his hands on the controls, while he, Kosiya, sat behind, supporting him, and together they made their painful way back to Gahini.

A decrepit lorry was found to take Joe to Kabale hospital to get help from Len Sharp. At one in the morning in a cold mountain mist the lorry went out of control, turned over on its side and Joe, badly wounded as he was, landed in the road in a heap. He eventually arrived to find Len on safari, so instead he instructed the African dressers who anaesthetized and treated him. Over the next ten days in hospital he had time to reflect and pray, determining to ask forgiveness of the older missionary Constance Hornby for not heeding what she had said about hunting. Certainly her comment 'I don't mind what happens to you . . .' had come back to haunt him, and as time went on he stopped hunting for glory and killed only for the pot. In later years he loved to let his grandchildren feel where the leopard's eye-tooth had made a big indentation in the top of his skull. Algie Stanley Smith commented in *Ruanda Notes* after Geoff Holmes had been similarly wounded, 'Hunting leopards is dangerous work; but no man who can shoot could refuse to risk even life itself to save these helpless people, children mostly, from such a treacherous foe.' But what sport they had in the process! Joe, Geoff and Dr Len Sharp all loved the excitement of hunting big game. Len was credited with the record for killing the biggest water-buck of his time, and a photograph of a leopard skin shot by Joe bears this inscription, signed by him: 'This is the skin of a very fine leopard, shot by me at night from the car at Rukira village. The skin was later taken by me to Rowland Ward's in London for registration and it turned out to be the world's record, and is reported in the latest official records. This skin was later presented by me to HRH the King of the Belgians and is in one of two cases in the Brussels Natural History Museum.'

By November, Joe's last bandage had come off. He continued struggling against the problems of Gahini. In one distressing episode, the government porters who had been repeatedly replacing the government supply of dried beans (which they carried up to the hospital) with stones, and keeping the food for themselves, had to be punished after several warnings. The theft was reported to Joe at the worst possible time – just at the end of a Sunday morning service. There was nothing for it but to sit the men round the hospital veranda, each with his load in front of him. 'Then with Kosiya helping I gave them a sermon about the evils of stealing, especially from sick, defenceless people, and I reminded them about my warning. The bags were opened and every man found with stones in his load was beaten by the headman, before all the others. It was a horrible business, but sin is sin, and I think it had a salutary effect. Long afterwards when the famine was over and God blessed us in a new way, I spoke of this episode in church and said I never wanted to do it again and asked them to forgive me.' But the famine and its terrible effects upon the people was getting him down:

I had begun to have a certain nightmare which has often repeated itself. It came from having to walk round every day among the famine patients who were all sleeping on grass on the floors because we had no beds yet in the hospital. Patients had a way of following me and pulling at my bare arms with their cold dry fingers, crying for food. One night in my dream I looked round to see a mother with a baby with its face half eaten away with yaws. When it got me down too much I would run down to the lake or just lie in my canvas canoe and float on the water in the evening; or I would rush out to the wild bush-country at the back of Gahini, and sit and watch the game till it was dark, and talk to God about it in prayer; or sometimes I would do a little hunting to get exercise.

By December things were desperate. The Belgian Government, short-staffed and ill-prepared, was unable to send enough food for the thousands of starving people arriving at Gahini, some of whom if strong enough would try to press on northwards to the fertile areas of Uganda some one hundred to two hundred miles further on. One day Joe found a small child sitting crying beside its dead mother; soon other dead bodies were found on the site. Joe wrote to

Decie that he longed to run away, anywhere, to get away from it all, but he knew that God had put them there for just this time of need.

And yet what could they do with no adequate funding or resources? Gahini had become a food distribution centre, and Joe and Bert Jackson travelled back and forth along the lake in the boat given by the Officers' Christian Union, collecting government supplies of beans and maize from Kigali. But even the beans and maize they gave out were raw and hard. There was no firewood to cook for all these people. They did manage to buy milk from the Batutsi who herded their cows around the lake, and that saved some of the children. Joe described the situation in *Ruanda Notes*: 'At dawn shadowy forms can be seen coming up the hill as they do every day to beg for food. It is impossible to describe the terrible spectacle provided by the starving patients who flock to the hospital every day. They crawl to the hospital from miles around . . . Many are covered with ulcers, filthily dirty, their toes and fingers rotting with jiggers. As they lie on the ground, with flies crawling over them, one's heart is broken when one thinks that for these almost inhuman beings, Christ died.'

And in his diary Joe recorded, 'The atmosphere is appalling. I often have to get out to breathe. Then this afternoon something came over me. I had to run down to the old thatched house down the hill through the lines of people collecting to be fed to consult with Algie. I felt defeated and disgusted. It makes my blood boil . . . why all this cruelty . . . I could wring someone's neck! But whose?' As he commented later:

It was the cry of a distracted person, I know, but it was also the cry of a suffering world going up to God. It would kill me if I tried to carry it myself. There was only one who could carry this load, and he allowed it to kill him before rising again. But I was slow to see this. I said to Algie, 'This whole business is defeating me, Algie. Come and have a last look.' He came up and we walked once more down the lines of men and women silently waiting with their arms stretched out. Most were infected with yaws and jiggers, children too crippled to walk crawling with food baskets held in their mouths. 'A suppurating mass of humanity,' I wrote.

Algie came with me to inspect the daily burying of bodies in the clay pits in the brick-fields. A terrible sight met us. They were shovelling earth onto the bodies, but one body we saw was still breathing. We shouted to them to stop and I jumped down to get the man out and called for his relatives. A poor woman came down and sat among the dead holding her dying husband in her arms. She had a deep gash in her scalp where she had been hit with a stick that morning while stealing, up in the village. Algie and I had both had enough. He went back to pack his lorry. The Stanley Smiths had given five months of unstinted brotherly love to us.

In their place, a retired lady called Mrs Wilkinson (known as Mrs Winnie), whose son Leslie was later to be Chairman of the Ruanda Council, came out from England to help at Gahini for a while. Pondering the horrors of that time, Joe wrote in his autobiography, 'I tried to analyse why it was I felt this suffering so much. Was I different from others? Or was I making too much fuss about it? I don't remember often having this feeling of boiling anger in England. But that is how I feel when I see suffering or unfairness.' Now, feeling more and more helpless in the face of the increasing suffering of starvation and disease, Joe, sensitive, frustrated, exhausted, and without Decie or any of his family to help him bear the load, saw his first Christmas at Gahini come and go.

The new year, 1929, brought continued difficulties, among them another accident in which, returning from a confinement, Joe fell over the side of a rickety bridge into the river with his motorbike on top of him. But the biggest trial continued to be the frustration of never being able to care for people properly, or to do building work as it ought to be done, due to lack of resources. For Joe, a perfectionist who enjoyed doing things well, this was not easy to bear. Later he came to see that God was bringing him and the others to the end of themselves so that they would be ready to receive an outpouring of his Holy Spirit in revival. But for the moment, horror was added to horror. One night Bert and Joe heard what they thought was a jackal at the end of the garden. With torch and shotgun they searched but found nothing. The strange noise went on from time to time and then stopped. Next morning they found a completely naked man who had crawled as far as the garden and died. At about the same time Bert called Joe to his bathroom one night as there was a dreadful smell and something in his bathtub. They pulled aside a sheet and found a living skeleton of a boy, just alive, who had crawled into the bath, pulled a sheet over himself and gone to sleep. He was covered from head to foot in sores.

In February, Joe wrote in *Ruanda Notes*, 'The famine becomes worse and worse, hundreds of people are dying or packing up and leaving the country. The hills around are full of empty kraals and one cannot go far in any direction without seeing corpses lying by the roadside. The conditions at the hospital are ghastly and very difficult to deal with. We have had to open our doors to the flood of starving and diseased people.' On 16 February 1929 Joe wrote a strongly worded letter to the Belgian Resident in Kigali but got no response. The annual pre-Christmas rains had failed, so all hope of a crop was gone and it was decided that Joe should set off for Kampala, the capital of Uganda, to seek help there, leaving Bert and Yosiya Kinuka, the head hospital assistant, in charge. Joe also needed attention for a corneal ulcer in one eye, so a visit to Kampala seemed a doubly good idea. He reached Kampala in two days on his Triumph, arriving on Friday 8 March, and stayed with a Christian business friend, a Mr Warren.

Unknown to Joe, the very day of his arrival the *Uganda Herald* had published an article entitled *Famine in the Congo*, saying, 'We are not aware whether any application for assistance has been made to the Uganda Government.' It added that Ruanda was their next-door neighbour and should they not go to their help? Reading the article over the weekend, both Joe and his friend had the same idea: they must launch a famine appeal. Arrangements were quickly made. Warren would be Treasurer, Dr Albert Cook agreed to act as Secretary to the appeal, and Bishop Willis, Bishop of Uganda, was to be Chairman. Joe's task was to write the appeal for the newspapers.

A full-page article appeared in Uganda on 22 March. In it Joe gave credit to the efforts of the Belgian Government, but he wrote strongly about the Uganda Government's prohibition of the passage of food over the border and of stopping Ruandans from buying food in Uganda. Describing the people of eastern Ruanda as now effectively shut up in a trap, he gave harrowing descriptions of the sufferings he had witnessed: 'The country is littered with corpses; one finds women and children lying helpless in the road, perhaps to be eaten by hyenas before they are even dead . . .' He ended with a phrase that in his inexperience he did not realize had associations with atrocities in the Congo: 'Even Ruanda, one of the most beautiful parts of Africa, can have a famine. Will you help to heal this open sore?' It was the very phrase Livingstone had used about the slave trade years earlier.

Visiting Dr Albert Cook and his wife Katherine, Joe poured out some of his concerns as they discussed the relief fund. Suddenly, to his amazement, after a whispered consultation with his wife, Dr Cook turned to Joe and announced that they wished to give him their old Model T Ford car for Gahini. They had been about to sell it that very day, but felt it would make a real contribution, facilitating the transport of food and medicines and generally improving communication. Joe was thrilled: 'I could hardly finish my lunch. I wanted to go immediately and look at it! I thanked them profusely. It was an open model with a folding hood. It had carried the Cooks many thousands of miles, but to me it was a Rolls Royce! I always revelled in an open car. I wanted to go out and stroke it!' Dr Cook also examined Joe's eye and pronounced that there was a considerable loss of sight which would sadly not be restored. Joe told him of his previous experience of miraculous healing while at Cambridge and said he felt he should once more ask God to heal him completely. The two men prayed together, and from that time on the eye improved until eventually the sight was totally restored.

Next day, with the Ford loaded up with food, medical supplies and tree seedlings, and his motorbike stowed in the open back, Joe sped happily through the game country enjoying the view from his lofty seat: 'It was one of those delicious days when I just sang for joy as I sped along. The phenomenal clearance of the old Ford would easily avoid all the anthills in the road, and I knew that the harder you drive a Ford the better it goes! Roll on the day in a year's time, I thought, when Decie would be coming out to join me. I also had beside me a little yelping puppy, a pedigree Airedale that friends in Nairobi had sent me when they heard of the loss of my first dog.' But calling in at the tin mines at Bujumo, 20 miles from Gahini, Joe met with a rebuff. The manager's wife had just been staying with the Belgian Resident in Kigali, and she reported that he was very angry about Joe's article. This was the start of some 'stormy days of misunderstanding', and as Joe recalls, 'At that time for several months I began to get haunted by failure and fears, a lot of it unnecessary worry. Surely, I thought, there must be a place of rest in Jesus in a deeper place of understanding of the victorious life? As I look back on those days I see the hand of God in it all, bringing me to know more about that place of rest.'

The English press picked up Joe's article. *The Times* of 16 April 1929 published a full column under the title *A Stricken Land*, adding a preface about a recent visit of Bishop Willis to Ruanda giving weight to what Joe had written, and moving Joe's last remark about the 'open sore' to the beginning. *The Times Weekly* of 1 April published an independent article from information provided by their correspondent in Nairobi and quoting Joe's name, and on 4 April the *Cambridge Daily News* repeated the account adding a paragraph about Joe's and his father's connections with Cambridge under the heading *Cambridge Man's Lone Hand in Famine-Stricken Area*. Soon the acute needs of Ruanda were taken up by the international press in many parts of the world.

The situation was raised in Parliament in London on 22 April, when Sir Robert Thomas, Liberal member for Anglesey, asked the Secretary of State for the Colonies if he would make a statement regarding the situation created by the 'influx into Uganda of famine-stricken natives from Ruanda', and what degree of co-operation there was with the Belgian authorities in coping with the situation. Questions were also asked in the Belgian Parliament, and statements were made about the steps that Belgium was taking to help relieve the famine, including cancelling the Resident's leave, and pointing out how much more they were doing than the previous German regime had achieved.

Joe arrived back at Gahini to find it in the midst of a deluge of rain. 'The result was disastrous. Sun-dried bricks were melting away, my roads and flowers were being washed into the lake, the pit latrines dug with such labour and insistence from us were tumbling in (one poor man was buried alive), and the crowds of famine patients were huddled shivering in the cold and rain – no firewood, no blankets, no food.' Twenty people died in one day. It seemed that things could get no worse. Almost at once a messenger arrived from Algie Stanley Smith in Kabale with news that the first gifts were beginning to come in from the appeal, but still they battled on against the many diseases which constantly attacked the weakened population: malaria and tick fever, typhoid, bacillary dysentery and alastrim, a disease which simulated the dreaded smallpox.

Joe was more and more depressed. 'I began to feel that the Roman Catholics were making capital out of my letter to the press and that I was in real danger of being asked to leave the country. My call to Ruanda seemed suddenly to be falling about my ears. Prayer and faith seemed to become unreal.' He managed to catch a brief meeting with Algie who put new heart into him with good news of the response to the appeal. They prayed together, and Joe 'sailed back home once more in my chariot with the hood down breathing the elixir of the African game plains.' As he wrote to Decie, 'I am making a real effort to do more Bible teaching . . . as I look back over the past year it has been one colossal maze of new things, excitements, difficulties, death and disease, and an overwhelming sense of the power of the devil . . . but we have the Truth, the Victory, and a personal living Saviour . . .'

And indeed at about this time the tide at last began to turn. The Belgian newspaper *L'Essor Coloniale* published an article by M. Jaspar, the Prime Minister and Minister of Colonies, saying that he had given orders for doctors to be loaned from the neighbouring Congo and announcing a huge grant for the making of new roads and for transport. He thanked the CMS Ruanda Mission for co-operating in the alleviation of the famine, and commented too on the response to *The Times* article, saying that it was proof of goodwill and international brotherhood. In London a steady stream of gifts came in from *The Times* offices to the CMS. The first cable arrived in Kabale on 14 May: 'London cables Ruanda relief draw pounds 250 specialize medical.' For several months gifts kept coming in.

After this the whole country began to be opened up and transformed. Swiss and Italian mountain-road engineers came and surveyed roads up to all the previously inaccessible food-bearing districts, and some amazing roads were made as tourist attractions. A Belgian official assured Joe that despite all the trouble his article caused, it had been the means of waking them up, and had brought about the rapid development of the whole country. And to Joe too it seemed that God was indeed behind it all, as shortly afterwards a friend of the Mission gave a very large sum of money which made possible the opening up of four new mission stations based on those new roads.

9

1929–1930: New Life from the Grave

One of those who had volunteered to go to Gahini from Kabale in 1928 was Yosiya Kinuka. He had come as head hospital assistant, with Dorokasi (Dorcas) his wife. As the physical needs caused by the famine began to ease slightly, Joe and Yosiya developed a system of Bible teaching, Joe reading a short Bible passage, the crowd repeating it line by line, Joe commenting as best he could in Lunyaruanda and Yosiya then explaining in his own words what Joe had said. Like this, the Bible largely spoke for itself and first-class mastery of Lunyaruanda was not essential. Later they began also to use a blackboard to bring home the teaching with pictures – an early form of visual aid. For example, for Psalm 40 verse 2, 'He brought me up out of a horrible pit', showing first a pin man at the bottom of a long deep pit shaking his fist at God; then the same man praying and crying to God for help; and then again kneeling at the foot of the cross. The Africans would gather round the board afterwards, explaining the message to each other from the pictures. But despite the work he put in on all this with Joe, Yosiya acknowledged afterwards that at that time he himself had not yet found that place at the foot of the cross.

Things were still far from easy at Gahini although money was now coming in from the famine appeal. Disease was still rampant, food was short with the beginning of the long dry season and the staff were overworked and tired. They were also becoming discontented, partly because of Joe's insistence that they were to be first and foremost evangelists, and not only hospital workers. This meant among other things that they were paid on an equal footing with the church teachers, when they thought they should be paid more. So while Joe and Bert Jackson sought ways for hospital and church to work ever more closely together, the staff, Yosiya included, became increasingly restless, remembering their time at Kabale where the roles of church and hospital workers were more clearly defined. Joe had seen the drawbacks of that pattern, and was working towards a new model of *Dispensaire-Chapelle-Ecoles* or church first-aid posts, where people would see a clear testimony of church and hospital working in partnership, but so far his ideas received little response. Often as he put heart and soul into expounding something from the Bible, he would see his listeners' minds far away on their wages, and when he looked round for Yosiya's support, he too could be seen looking as uninvolved as possible away at the back of the room. Looking back and laughing with Joe over the situation some time later, Yosiya likened it to a struggle to push a car that wouldn't go up hill. The only real hope was new power in the engine. And Joe began to see that all his good ideas which must often have tried the patience of his African helpers, needed a new infilling of the Holy Spirit if they were to work.

Eventually the workers had had enough. One hot afternoon in June 1929 as Joe sat on the veranda of the thatched house where he and Bert lived, a silent line of hospital workers filed round the corner and stood sullenly in front of him, each with his hospital uniform neatly folded, while their spokesman announced their intention to leave. Joe knew there was no point in discussing again the contentious issues of pay and the need for hospital workers to do evangelistic work. Exhausted himself after a hard morning at the hospital and with no reserves of patience left, he simply told them all to go if they wished, at which they dropped their bundles at his feet and left as silently as they had come. In fact they didn't stop working at the hospital, but the situation remained uneasy and strained. Despite this discouragement, a few days later Joe set off by boat into the sunset along the lake and next day arranged with the Belgian official in Kigali for a small plot of land on a hilltop called Ndera, where under a glorious umbrella acacia tree a new dispensary-church was soon to be built.

The pressures they were under led to a new burden for prayer, and as Joe described in a letter home to his mother, 'We have started having a prayer meeting with some of the leading Christians out of doors at dawn on Thursday morning, on the hillside. It is a wonderful time to pray.' They also started daily Bible studies. At 2 p.m. everyone stopped work for the *isaa munani* – the 2 p.m. teaching time – when, led by Joe, Bert or Kosiya Shalita, they followed through the great themes of Scripture as traced out in the Scofield Bible, a series of studies which lasted for years and were eventually published and reprinted many times under the title *Every Man a Bible Student*. Just as on the physical level the dry hill of Gahini was slowly being transformed as Joe laid out paths and planted beautiful trees – flame of the forest, eucalyptus, thorn-trees, flowering cacti – so too in the spiritual realm shoots of fresh new life were beginning to appear.

At about the same time another key person arrived at Gahini: Blasio Kigozi, a young Muganda who had volunteered to take charge of a small boys' school of 15 pupils which had started at Gahini but closed during the worst of the famine. Bert Jackson wrote about Blasio's arrival in *Ruanda Notes*, 'We praise God for him; it is no small sacrifice for a rich young fellow to leave a land of plenty and prosperity like Uganda for this famine-stricken area. Fifteen boys. What a meagre handful! Yet among them there may be some who shall be so utterly yielded to the Holy Spirit, so filled with the power of God, that all Ruanda may through them ring with the goodness of the Saviour, and thousands be brought to his feet.' As Joe commented, these proved to be prophetic words.

Joe had personal worries at this time. It seemed that the devil was beating him with several sticks at once. One was Decie's health – she was suffering from arthritis following a bout of German measles and was having to rest in bed. Joe began to doubt if she would be fit enough to cope with the rough life of Gahini. Surely the CMS would never pass Decie for service in Africa. This led Joe to wonder if he had been right to propose to her when he did. Then in September Joe failed his first language exam which he took in Kabale, an additional worry as a rule of the CMS was that marriage could not be sanctioned until that first exam was out of the way. And finally he was worried, and felt that Decie's family were too, that he would not be able to support her adequately once they were married. Joe was exhausted and overwrought. He wrote to Decie, 'I think in many ways this is one of the heaviest and blackest moments of my life. The Lord is as real as ever, but I just cannot see an inch ahead. I often feel that my witness for Christ must be almost nix. I am just trying all the more to give the Lord absolutely everything, and then to praise him, and wait for his guiding hand.' In the meantime he set off for Kampala for a much-needed holiday.

While there, an unexpected meeting took place, which many would pinpoint as the beginning of the revival: Joe's meeting with the Muganda Christian, Simeon Nsibambi, outside Namirembe Cathedral in September 1929. The significance of this meeting had its roots far back in the life of the church both in Britain and in Uganda, which need to be explained. As we have already seen, in matters of life and faith Joe was always eagerly looking for reality, for 'the Highest' and for the victorious life. It was this that he had missed in some of the churches he had visited in Bournemouth as a young man; it was this that had led him into the evangelical CICCU at Cambridge with its clear belief in the Bible as the word of God, rather than to the liberal Student Christian Movement (SCM) from which CICCU had split off in 1910. Back in 1920 he had gone with his CICCU friends to a big SCM conference in Glasgow, but had noted in his diary that there was spiritually something missing in some of the talks, commenting later, 'It was that rare thing *reality* which we missed even though one of the addresses was on 'God, the Supreme Reality'. Similarly with the confident and sometimes cruel discernment of the young, he and his friends would assess visiting speakers – many of them missionaries home on leave or else retired – who addressed the CICCU students, as either having, or sadly no longer having 'it'. This 'it' was the reality based on the forgiveness won by Christ on the cross, or as Joe illustrated the point: 'When the "I" and the "T" come together, that is when the "I" comes to the cross, to Calvary, then we find "IT".'

Even within the evangelical wing of the church there were those who sought a deeper reality and a deeper commitment. Many, including eager CICCU students, flocked to England's beautiful Lake District for the annual Keswick Convention. 'Keswick' spirituality, expounded here, sought not only a fresh apprehension of Christ crucified, but also a deeper filling with the Holy Spirit, a 'second blessing', a more thoroughgoing and continuous surrender to him. And within the Church Missionary Society, one of the more evangelical of Britain's great missionary societies, there had been divisions over the issue of liberal versus conservative interpretation of the Bible. This had led to the

splitting off of a separate group called the Bible Church-
men's Missionary Society in 1922. It had also meant that
the Ruanda Mission, which had originally been a development of the CMS's work, but financed separately by Doctors Sharp and Stanley Smith because of the CMS's lack of
resources at the time, decided eventually in 1926 to set up
its own council with a much clearer conservative basis than
that of its parent mission, the CMS.

All these differences of understanding and vision in the
parent church and mission were inevitably reflected in the
Anglican Church of Uganda. As a result of the Protestant
victory over Catholics and Muslims in the troubles around
King Mwanga's court in the 1890s, this had become the
dominant church in colonial Uganda. The Pilkington Revival of 1893 was an early attempt, influenced by the
Keswick movement, to assert the priority of the spiritual
over the political and social life in the church (C Harford
Battersby, *Pilkington of Uganda*. Quoted in Kevin Ward's
article, 'Obedient Rebels', *Journal of Religion in Africa* 19,
3 (1989), p. 195). But the different understandings and
resulting tensions remained. In 1928 Mabel Ensor, an Irish
nurse working at Mengo Hospital, Kampala, resigned from
the CMS and formed her own fellowship, the Mengo
Gospel Church, as a protest against the worldliness of the
Church of Uganda.

Joe had met Mabel during his brief stay in Kampala when
he first arrived in Africa. He starts his autobiographical
account *Quest for the Highest* with a description of their
meeting: 'You will never do anything for God in Uganda',
she had firmly told Joe, 'if you don't come out of that building' – pointing defiantly at Namirembe Cathedral as she
spoke. Joe had been talking to her about the liberal/conser-
vative divergence within the CMS, and how the Ruanda
Mission had remained as part of the CMS but with its own
governing council and clearly biblical basis of faith. Mabel,

who favoured making a complete break, poured out to Joe her concerns about the nominal faith of those who flocked into the cathedral and about the double standards practised by many of them. She invited Joe to speak to her Bible class that Sunday, and among the young men listening eagerly to what he had to say was Simeon Nsibambi, the older brother of Blasio Kigozi.

Now Joe was in Kampala again, and on Sunday morning he joined the crowd going up to the cathedral for the morning service. As he described, 'I walked through the old sun-dried brick archway at the top of the hill and there, opposite the entrance of the Synod Hall, was a man in a dark suit standing beside his motorbike. It was Simeon Nsibambi. He spotted me and ran out to greet me. He said how much he had enjoyed that time when I addressed Miss Ensor's class and asked if I had any more to tell them. I said I was looking for a new infilling of the Holy Spirit and for the victorious life. He warmed to this as we talked.' For some time Joe had been praying that God would lead him to a really saved African with whom he could have deep fellowship. Now here was this rich young Muganda in government service who had committed himself joyfully to Christ previously but was aware of something missing in the Uganda church and in himself. Over the next two days he and Joe spent unhurried time going through the Bible together using Scofield's notes on the Holy Spirit and praying for the fullness of the Spirit in their own lives.

What they received was greater than anything Joe had imagined. As he described it many times in later years, it seemed that 'God in his sovereign grace met with me and brought me to the end of myself and thought fit to give me a share of the power of Pentecost.' Like the two disciples on the way to Emmaus, the hearts of these two men 'burnt within them' as the risen Christ drew near and revealed himself to them in a new way.

Regretfully they tore themselves away from this special time together. Simeon went back to his job in the Public Health Department, although he was soon to leave it and devote himself full-time to evangelistic work, and Joe went on to Nairobi where he was encouraged by a visit from the Belgian Consul-General who told him of the appreciation of the Belgian Government for the help the CMS had rendered during the Ruanda famine. He also had the fun of taking delivery of a new safari hospital car for transporting essential drugs and equipment for Gahini. He loved this sort of thing: 'It was an exhilaration to be purring up into the Highlands to over eight thousand feet behind six cylinders. I think one enjoyed Africa more in the days of semi-open cars.'

Back in Kampala Joe was surprised when a lady missionary asked him, 'What have you done to Nsibambi? He's gone mad and is going round everywhere asking people if they are saved. He's just left my gardener!' She told Joe in no uncertain terms that Africans were not ready for teaching on the fullness of the Spirit, a view which other bewildered missionaries were to share. Joe returned to Gahini where there was encouragement on various fronts. As he put it, 'With the new year came a breath of new hope. Gahini began to rise from the grave.' Bert Jackson and Cecil Verity, a new recruit from Cambridge, were getting on with building the hospital; Miss Hill, the Editorial Secretary of *Ruanda Notes* visiting from London, was able to report that 'Gahini has come through the ordeal and has reached the stage where real advance can be made' and, most cheering of all, there were several genuine and life-changing conversions including two local Tutsi chiefs both of whom had been patients in the hospital.

The time for Joe and Decie's wedding was drawing near. Joe had already had to face a big disappointment about where they would live. He had hoped to build a new house at Gahini, but the old thatched house where the other missionaries lived was becoming so unsafe that Algie had decided that Joe must re-roof it first before beginning on his own home. There wasn't enough time to do both, and Joe had to resign himself to his and Decie's moving into a small new nurses' house near the hospital which he had almost completed but which wouldn't after all be needed for nurses as soon as had been thought. Later Joe was able to write, 'A thousand times I have thanked God for helping me to "break" over that. How often I have found that when one breaks, God has something better which he has been waiting to give you. That hilltop house became our home-from-home in Africa, and I began to build another for the nurses and lady workers further down the hill.'

On Thursday 24 April, his language exam finally behind him, Joe was ready to set off to meet Decie at Nairobi when a new series of trials occurred. First he discovered that somebody had left the car ignition on for several days so the battery was flat. Eventually a new battery was obtained from Kigali, but his departure was delayed and he set off on the Friday evening intending to drive through the night. The rain was so heavy and the roads so bad that the car packed up again, only to reveal that the canvas flap at the back had come open and Joe's attaché case with all his letters and papers, and most precious of all his Bible, were lost. And when, hungry and exhausted, he came to eat the sandwiches which had been carefully prepared for his planned departure the previous day, he found they had gone bad in the heat and had to be thrown away untasted.

He spread his bed in the dark in the back of the car and knelt there to pray. One by one he brought all his burdens to God at the cross – his worries about Decie and whether she would cope with Africa, his lack of forgiveness for the person who had left the ignition turned on, his anger at the things he had lost. Then, as he described, 'Like Christian in *Pilgrim's Progress* my load was lifted from off my shoulders and it rolled and rolled, down into the pit and was gone; and I went to sleep resting in the sinner's place. That night was a landmark in my spiritual pilgrimage. As with Jacob, it had been my "Peniel" and I had seen God face to face.'

In Kampala he had some time with Simeon Nsibambi: 'I had arranged with Nsibambi to have some more times to read and pray over our Bibles when I came in to Kampala. He was often there to meet me just at the time I arrived at the end of my journey. He seemed to have a way of knowing the time even though I had not let him know. We met in the small room at the back of the Synod Hall at Namirembe, and he brought some Baganda friends. We met in the late afternoon, and there were thirty-five in all. Nsibambi was gathering around him a little team of those whose hearts God had touched, who went out preaching and doing personal work with him, especially one, Yusufu Mukasa. This was the first "Friday meeting" at Namirembe, and these meetings for fellowship and prayer are still being held in the same hall every Friday.' Unlike Mabel Ensor, who broke off and set up her own small Gospel mission, Nsibambi shared Joe's vision of remaining within the larger church and witnessing to it from within.

Because of continuing heavy rain, Joe went on by train to Nairobi: 'I walked up and down that long Nairobi station platform on 9 May waiting for the first puff of smoke to appear over the Athi plains. I had my last prayer of dedication and the great train steamed in. There were those brief moments when the Sharps, who had escorted Decie from England, faded away and left the carriage to us, and the two and a half years of our separation came to an end, and months of Satan's taunts. Decie looked more than ever beautiful and very happy.' The wedding was on 19 May, 1930, in Namirembe Cathedral, where later that day Joe and Decie placed the flowers of the wedding bouquet on the graves of Mackay, Pilkington and Bishop Hannington, Uganda pioneers. The reception was at Makindye, Dr and Mrs Cook's lovely home on the hilltop overlooking Lake Victoria. Decie's sister Vera, already married and living near Nairobi, was Decie's honorary bridesmaid and wrote home to Mrs Tracey: 'It was an inspiration for her to be married from the Cooks' home. They are so very much the origin and centre of the Uganda medical work . . . Everyone admired Dec immensely, saying she was the prettiest bride Kampala had ever seen.'

Dr and Mrs Schofield (he was assistant to Dr Cook at the CMS Mengo hospital) had given them a wonderful wedding present: 'For our honeymoon they sent a tent, complete with everything necessary for camping – bedding, food and their own cook – down to the shore of a small lake beside Lake Victoria, Nabugabo, where it was pitched beneath huge tropical trees where monkeys and birds chattered and sang all day long.' They were given an Alsatian dog as well, whom they called Jasper. Joe loved that dog, and it shared their honeymoon with them, a family joke being that there were more photographs of Jasper on the honeymoon than of Decie. Then, as Joe described, 'Finally on the 3rd of June, at the end of the rainy season with Gahini bright with flowers, we drove up to our new home. Mrs Winnie had prepared an afternoon tea table on the veranda of the old thatched house, ready to greet us, just as she would if we were calling on her on a June afternoon in an English garden.'

10

1931–1932: A Time of Fruitfulness

Now began a time of growth and encouragement for the
Ruanda Mission and for Joe and Decie personally. By the
end of its first decade, the Mission had established hospi-
tals, schools and churches in and around two bases:
Kabale in south-west Uganda and Gahini in eastern
Ruanda. Now, still under the firm leadership of Dr Leonard Sharp and Dr Algie Stanley Smith, there was, as Joe
wrote, 'a spirit of adventure for God, given by His Holy
Spirit, that caused us to claim in faith four new sites for
mission stations, covering the whole of Ruanda-Urundi'.
First, a precipitous road led them to the hill of Shyira, near
Ruhengiri in north-west Ruanda; next, 'another light was
set on a hill for God' at Kigeme in the south. Not long
afterwards two more sites were found – this time at
Matana and Buhiga, both in Urundi. Jim Brazier, Bert and
Frances Jackson and others pioneered at Shyira, setting up
a dispensary soon to be developed into full medical work
by Doctor Norman James, while high on the beautiful hilltop at Kigeme, Geoffrey Holmes and his new wife
Ernestine started work living in a little grass hut which
more often than not was inundated by rain. Soon crowds
were coming for Christian instruction, and buildings
began to go up. Meanwhile Joe and Decie continued to
work at Gahini, Decie helping on the medical side and

with the hospital accounts. The urgent need was for Spirit-filled Africans to help at the new outposts.

At Gahini the daily Bible teaching at staff prayers and the *isaa munani* (2 p.m. teaching time) went on, but with a new sense of urgency, and Joe and Decie also tried holding an extra time of fellowship with the hospital staff after supper in their dining room. But as Joe put it, 'There was no spark of new life yet, and Yosiya still sat at the back keeping out of my way.' Praying together for Yosiya, Joe and Blasio Kigozi came up with the idea of sending him to Kampala (where he was eager to go) to see Simeon Nsibambi, Blasio's brother. Joe paid his fare. While he was there, Yosiya and Simeon had long conversations about the bad spirit in the hospital at Gahini. 'The spirit in the hospital is bad because of sin in your own heart', Nsibambi told Yosiya. At last in the lorry on the way back to Gahini, Yosiya acknowledged his sin and yielded to Christ. By the time he walked up the hill to Joe and Decie's house, people were gathering round him realising that something momentous had happened. The whole expression of his face was changed.

Yosiya's conversion was a turning point. From now on, he and Blasio became fast friends, praying and planning eagerly with Joe. As Yosiya testified, 'Now we realize that we have been told by our Lord to preach and to heal . . . There has been a very great change between us and Dr Church. We realized that it was because of sin that we did not work with him, and that we were on the wrong side.' Their faith and witness began to reach others on the hospital staff. One, Paulo Gahundi, the hospital dresser with whom Joe had done his first ward round at Gahini, turned strongly against Yosiya after his conversion, making endless complaints against him. But one night there was a knock on Joe's door. Yosiya stood outside smiling as the tall figure of Paulo stooped to come in. They had had a serious talk together, in the course of which Paulo had come to repent of his opposition to Christ and to ask his forgiveness. Now he had come to ask for leave to go to Kigali where the gospel had never yet been preached, to tell people about Christ and to call them to repentance.

The example of Paulo, the aristocratic Mututsi, preaching in Kigali market place inspired others at Gahini. A motto was chosen: 'Every man an evangelist'. Soon Erifazi, a senior member of the hospital staff working in the operating theatre, repented publicly and was converted. He too asked for leave to go to his home far away in central Ruanda to preach the gospel there. What would become of the work of the hospital if this sort of thing continued? But God was in control. Already a double-sized intake was being trained in order to have dispenser-evangelists for the village church and first-aid centres, so there were people ready to step in to fill the gaps. In May Erifazi returned, full of enthusiasm, and offered to go as a missionary to a small tribe living on the Tanganyika (now Tanzania) border where mosquitoes and malaria were rife – an answer to prayer as Joe had been trying for two years to get a teacher to go there. A bricklayer, a carpenter, Joe's houseboy Muterahejuru and several others were similarly released to preach, often losing pay by doing so. Yosiya also clamped down on secret drinking among the staff. He told Joe that they used to drink at night and eat onions in the morning to cover up the smell. Indeed, as Yosiya commented in *Ruanda Notes*, 'Since Christmas there has been a very great change in the hospital.'

God's Holy Spirit was also beginning to work among the women at Gahini. Two high-class Tutsi women turned to Christ. One, a chieftainess called Maria Kamondo, lived 30 miles down the lake. Joe and others used to camp in her kraal when they went by boat to get famine relief food. Kamondo would come and talk to them, sitting under the flap of their tent as her cattle were being driven into the stockade for the night. After many talks she knelt and gave her heart to the Lord and became a changed woman, never looking back in spite of persecution. Another well-known Tutsi lady, Esiteri Nyirabatwa, with Egyptian-like features and long combed-up hair, was converted and baptized and devoted her life to winning the chiefs' wives for Christ and bringing the chiefs' children to the mission school.

But such enthusiasm inevitably attracted opposition, and not only from unbelievers. One regrettable source was the Roman Catholic Church. In a way this was not surprising, as Ruanda at that time was a Belgian protectorate and Belgium was a strongly Roman Catholic country. As Joe put it, 'Hardworking but bigoted Catholic priests had been in the country for about 27 years before we arrived and still had an almost pre-Reformation attitude towards any intrusion.' It was the done thing for chiefs to wear a Catholic medallion around their necks and they put pressure on their people not to listen to the Protestant missionaries, expecting them to accept the State religion without question. As the Ruanda Mission and the newly enthusiastic African Christians reached out into the countryside with medical and evangelistic outposts, so the Roman Catholics reacted understandably but most unfortunately. As Joe described: 'The game of chess continues. Roman Catholic churches are being built on all the hills around us; their aim is to swamp us and hem us in by sheer numbers, but we are moving out our "pawns", rejoicing that our King can never be "checkmated".'

It seemed clear to Joe and to his colleague Cecil Verity that, despite this unfortunate situation, they must continue to preach the gospel and the Word of life. They took care to avoid any open attack or polemic, and determined to rely solely on faithful Bible teaching of the love of God, on the healing ministry of the hospital which demonstrated that same love and was available to all, and on the spontaneous testimony of changed lives as patients and others responded to that love. As Joe wrote, 'A stream of patients who had been healed in hospital was beginning to permeate deeply into the country with the story of the love of God that they had learned . . . so the Gospel spread.' Previously, Christian adherence had not changed people's way of life. They were 'Christianized' but not converted. Now when a Catholic priest complained about the noisy singing of new Christians, he was shown a hut full of returned stolen hoes and told, 'When you can show something like this, we'll listen to your complaint.'

In September 1931, 65 people were confirmed at Gahini. Over 1,000 people were present in the new church building, its roof completed only two days before. The confirmation was preceded by dawn prayer meetings on Joe's veranda and a week's convention with special Bible teaching – such conventions were to become a feature of the Revival in years to come. In November something else happened which Joe saw as a vital link in the chain leading to Revival: the first copies of the New Testament in Lunyaruanda, painstakingly translated by Harold Guillebaud, reached Gahini. The hospital staff came asking to buy them on the very first evening, so eager to have them that they insisted they could not sleep without them. And at Christmas, over 2,000 people packed into the new church and outside it, many of them the readers or candidates for baptism of the 40 surrounding village churches. 'It is like living in the times of the Apostles here now,' Joe wrote home. 'Every baptized person knows full well that he is going out to meet persecution.'

As well as at Gahini, Joe was pursuing the goal of consecration and the Spirit-filled life more widely in the East African Church. He visited Kampala in September and, together with Simeon Nsibambi, arranged various meetings to this end – among them a two-day retreat for the ordinands' and lay readers' course at the Bishop Tucker Memorial Theological College, Mukono; another for members of the Makerere University College Students' Christian Union. His unorthodox approach did not go unnoticed by Bishop Willis: 'Good morning, Church,' he greeted him one morning, 'and what meeting have you got in my Diocese today?' In fact not everyone in the parent Church of Uganda was happy with what some saw as Joe and Simeon's 'holier than thou' approach, but Joe was convinced that the church desperately needed revival, and Simeon had remained within the Church to help make this a reality.

While Joe worked on and rejoiced in new birth and new life for many at Gahini and elsewhere, he was also rejoicing in birth and new life at a personal level, for back in March Decie had given birth to their first son, John Christian. And Gahini itself was blossoming with new life. Situated two degrees below the equator and at an altitude of 5,000 feet it had ideal growing conditions. Many English flowers grew profusely. Joe and Decie, both of whom loved plants and gardens, began to specialize in trees of all kinds, and avenues of cassia, jacaranda, cypress, kapok, eucalyptus and whispering fir were growing up, as well as the subtropical pepper trees which reminded them of the weeping willows beside the river in Cambridge. A Belgian passing one day commented, 'C'est tout à fait un parc – un parc anglais!' It was becoming a paradise.

Other visitors came too, and were impressed: Harold Guillebaud saw faces shining with the joy of the Lord, reflecting lives really changed by the Holy Spirit's power; and Dr Stanley Smith found the hospital full and a great and deep work going on there, adding, 'It was very impressive to me to come to Gahini and see the wonderful development in the 18 months since I was last there. A really lovely church crowns the hill, and the whole of the girls' work has come into being.'

Now the time had come for Joe and Decie to go home to England for Joe's first leave. To help to make this possible, Joe's brother Bill, who had now qualified as a doctor and taken his tropical medicine course in Belgium, fulfilled his promise and came out to Gahini to work in the hospital and to run it while Joe was away. Bill, fair and good-looking, younger than Joe, had been the wildest of the family as a boy. Now, tamed by the Holy Spirit, he was to prove a quiet and totally reliable support for Joe. On the journey out, still shattered by a broken engagement, he had written in the family circular letter of his thankfulness for his parents and his home: 'I am sure there are few happier homes in England than ours and I'm sure the secret is simply that we are one in Christ Jesus.' Commenting on his parents' ready sacrifice of first Mary, then Joe and himself to the mission field, he added, 'It is inevitable that we continue to break up and separate, but it will be wonderful if this letter continues to bind us together in intelligent prayer.' While Joe, the charismatic leader, would be more and more on the move as the years went by, Bill would provide an anchor for the medical work, first at Gahini and then at Buhiga in Urundi. Joe met him in Kabale, and after attending the big annual conference of CMS missionaries in Kampala they set off together for Gahini, arriving on 19 January 1932. Despite the idyllic surroundings, Bill was not impressed by what he found: 'I was startled', he wrote, 'by the terrible state of the hospital following the famine. The patients lit fires in the wards and the ceilings were black. The walls of the wards were infested with ticks, which carry the dreaded tick fever. Sanitation was almost absent as the sides of the verandas were lined with huge Canna lilies fertilised by the urine of the patients who used them at night. In the rocks below the doctor's house were heaps of bones of those who had died in the famine. Hyenas could be heard howling there most nights.'

White ants had wrought havoc with the buildings too.

Joe had done all he could; the state of the hospital buildings, in the providence of God, he could safely leave to his brother Bill, who relates: 'After a few weeks Joe and family left, leaving me in charge. The nurse also soon left, dissatisfied with the condition of the hospital, and due for furlough. She was succeeded by a new nurse from Ireland who told me in no uncertain terms that she would not tolerate the existing conditions. Dr Algie Stanley Smith turned up, and in him I found a tower of wisdom and strength. We started by removing the front verandas and unhygienic Canna lilies. I worked very hard building, attending to the sick, and installing the sanitary arrangements. I learnt later that my hidden African name was "the latrine digger ..." ' Joe had planted the banks of lilies as part of his scheme for beautifying Gahini. His brother, more down to earth, felt bound to rip them out.

Bill found a welcome sense of unity at Gahini, but noted too that although the church was large, 'Most were nominal Christians, turning up for the service on Sunday, but under their shirts they wore charms. There was much drinking and fights on Sunday evening, and on Monday morning I had to sew up head wounds.' The Revival had barely begun. Meanwhile Joe, Decie and little John Christian were on board the *Dunluce Castle* heading for England, and to Devon which for Decie was home.

11

1933–1935: Revival at Gahini

They arrived at Southampton on 24 April 1932 and were met by Decie's mother, Alice, who took them straight to the Tracey family home, The Gables, in the village of Willand. Decie's grandfather, Henry Eugene Flos Tracey, was a noted evangelical preacher, remarkable in his ability to bridge the gap between the Plymouth Brethren, who were dominant in the area at the time, and the established Church. Decie's father Eugene, a doctor and himself an only son, built a huge house, The Gables, 'to fill with little Traceys'. Sadly he died when Decie was very young, but he had fulfilled his ambition as Decima was the tenth child of eleven.

England was at its most beautiful. As Joe wrote, 'England seemed like a new country to me. After being abroad one realizes the luscious beauty of English Spring; there's nothing to touch it in Europe or Africa to my mind.' Joe and Decie were happy to be home again and to introduce John Christian to his grandparents. In July there was new rejoicing as their second son, David, conceived far away in the heart of Africa, was born in the same room at The Gables where Decie herself had been born. As Joe described, 'He was born during Keswick [the Convention] and I shall never forget getting the telegram just as I was going to speak at the huge missionary meeting. Mrs

Tracey could not have done more for Decie (who is her Benjamin), and us as a family.'

Edward and Florence Church were equally thrilled to meet their grandchildren. Edward proudly carried John Christian around, showing him off to their friends and amusing him by 'blowing open' the back of his presentation gold watch. They were no longer in the industrial parish of St Andrew the Less in Cambridge, but at Fen Ditton nearby, where Edward, now an Honorary Canon of Ely Cathedral and nearing retirement, had been offered the living of St Mary's church and the large and beautiful rectory with its garden going down to the river Cam. As Joe described, 'My father and mother could never cease thanking God for every corner of that old-world rectory with its wych elms and walled garden.' CICCU members still came over on their bikes for Sunday teas, and the paddock was one of the most sought-after positions from which to watch the Cambridge University boat races.

Coming there on his first leave from Gahini with Decie and John in 1932, this is what Joe found:

Fen Ditton grows on one, I find. It is home, but home in a broader sense – I find there not only the family, and the in-laws, but representatives of many other shows: CICCU, Ridley, Broads camps, etc., who have come to look upon our family as part of themselves. So one finds Mrs Ernest Young with her huge girls' squashes in the drawing room and her Rover car – very useful at times! – Robert Dodson quietly doing the boys' Bible class; Jack Collins cooking sausages with Wizzie in the kitchen on Sunday evenings; the phone continually in use; Geoffrey Young flying over twice a week waving to us from his aeroplane; R.R.Webster, the Ruanda secretary down for the weekend; Joan Cooper helping Wizz with the Crusaders – and so on.

While Decie looked after the children, Joe rushed up and down the country in his second-hand open Morris Oxford car, attempting to meet the many requests to speak about their work, about the famine in Ruanda, and in particular about revival and how God had met him and others, both black and white, when they had come to the end of themselves.

On 10 March 1933 they sailed back to Africa on the same ship as Joe's younger brother, Howard, now ordained, who was heading for Kenya where he was to work fruitfully with the CMS for many years, notably as chaplain in the Mau Mau camp at Athi River. A year after their arrival in England Joe and Decie were back at Gahini: 'We rounded the bend of the lake five miles from Gahini on April 27th at 4 p.m. and could see all the white buildings and galvanized iron roofs standing out in the sun . . . I hesitated a bit at the thought of entering into the fray again, but we had a great reception, David and John being the chief attractions.' There were other attractions too: two Alsatians, a Persian cat, Cuss the monkey, a tame golden-crested crane and – soon to be born – eight puppies. They all settled in happily and Joe, thanks to the improvements Bill had wrought to the hospital buildings, got straight down to the medical work.

The spiritual work was moving forward too. A few weeks before they had left for England, a great encouragement had come to the Ruanda Mission in the form of a gift from a Christian businessman, Mr Carr of Nairobi (father of Ernestine, now Mrs Holmes), of £500 a month for five years for the development of the four new sites in Ruanda-Urundi. The Stanley Smiths had moved to Kigeme to develop the medical work there, and the Holmeses, with Geoffrey now ordained, were back at Gahini, leading the church work together with Kosiya Shalita, now also ordained. Joe and Geoff didn't always find it easy to work together. With Yosiya Kinuka giving a lead at the hospital, many Africans were coming into an experience of salvation and challenging older Christians. Timetables both in hospital and school were being disrupted as revived Christian workers rushed off suddenly to witness to family or friends or stayed rapt in lengthy meetings. Geoff with his military background found the resulting enthusiasm and disorder hard to accept. Both he and Joe were prone to irritability and anger. Both had to learn to allow the Holy Spirit to deal with these things if revival was not to be hindered. As Joe put it, 'We were beginning to see that we had come as missionaries to bring light, but every now and then that light was turned round to shine on us.'

At about this time Joe sent home photographs of their beautiful surroundings – a view from the veranda looking

west over Lake Mohasi, the grass walk down the middle surrounded by marigolds and balsam, the home-made sundial; and the veranda itself shaded from the glare of the lake by purple bougainvillea and pale blue climbing potato creeper. With the photographs he wrote:

You may think sometimes when you look at these photos that Gahini is a beautiful sort of health resort. But do remember that the mission field is full of pitfalls and problems and differences. There are sleepless nights and burning hearts on every station, and it seems to me that these are the ways by which God brings us nearer to Himself. These six months have been a time of rethinking of missionary problems for me. The beautiful station, with orderly avenues and flowers, becomes unconsciously, but almost inevitably entwined with the self-made web of convention . . . [I am] striving for 'the life that is hid with Christ in God'.

Joe developed this idea of 'convention' in an entry in his personal diary – a cry from the heart which epitomizes the central struggle of his work:

I sometimes have glimpses of a life of pentecostal power, but I'm learning to abide and wait for an unconscious impelling which will send me forth perhaps on some more definite mission work. We are getting more and more conventionalized here. The scaffolding of convention is filling the picture and hiding the building, all too feeble in parts, behind it. My visions of co-operation, worked out with some pain and much prayer with Cecil are fading a bit [the Rev Cecil Verity was in charge of evangelists' training at Gahini]. It seems that the 'parish system' has such a hold on the C of E missionary mind that all unconsciously they drift into it. The Uganda church is the final result. A vast nominal Protestant mass of scaffolding with much paganism still behind it. Yosiya is my Timothy, and largely through him the whole hospital staff seems to have been really saved. If Geoff continues (unconsciously I think) his policy of departmentalizing the church side of the work I should not care to continue here. Life is too short and if the scaffolding spoils the building we should pull it down or start on a new building.

The Rev Lawrence Barham and his wife Julia visited from Kabale in August 1933, and he and Joe got down to important issues at Gahini and 'God began to weld us into a "team for two" for revival with its basis of real trust and openness at the Cross'. Lawrence, like Joe, had studied at Cambridge and he shared Joe's concern that 'everything should be *real*'. A teaching convention arranged by Lawrence Barham at Kabale in September, and a Convention for Ruanda Mission workers on an island on Lake Bunyoni which raised issues facing the growing church on how far the structures of the Anglican Church should be applied in Africa, were other important events. Joe and others were anxious lest these Anglican structures should hinder the work of God's Spirit; others feared the effects of increasing freedom and change. One result was an increasing turning to prayer. In October Joe wrote to the CICCU about prayer as the vital means by which we tune in to God and become channels for his power to flow through to man: 'We can work furiously, play games, learn languages, organize and build, but all will be only as chaff blown away in the wind if we are not tuned in . . .'

At Gahini as they prayed, there was an increasing sense of expectancy. Evangelistic teams were being trained and going out every weekend. Hospital staff workers were building themselves small thatched prayer huts as they felt the need to come apart and be alone with God. In November Joe wrote, 'There have been several cases of repentance among senior Christians. One brought back half a month's pay for paraffin stolen during the year, another brought 22 francs for stolen medicine . . . I believe a real move of the Spirit is coming.'

After Christmas, beginning on 27 December 1933, a five-day convention was held at Gahini for Bible teaching and prayer. At first there seemed to be little genuine response and, unknown to Joe, Geoffrey Holmes decided that the convention should continue for an extra day of prayer. The extra prayer meeting began in the church at 3 p.m. on the Saturday. In Joe's words:

> After half an hour of the usual formal prayers Kosiya slipped out and asked me to come. He said he could not stick it any longer; people praying beautiful long prayers, many of them hypocrites he knew who needed to be broken down before God. He wanted to ask Mr Holmes to stop the meeting. We agreed that nothing but the Spirit of God could break men's hearts . . . A remarkable thing happened a few minutes later. While everyone was bowed in prayer one of the African Christians got up and began confessing some sin he had committed, and then all sat up. It seemed as though a barrier of reserve had been rolled away. A wave of conviction swept through them all and for two and a half hours it continued, sometimes as many as three on their feet at once trying to speak . . . We had to stop them when it was dark at 6.30 p.m. Many laid themselves down that night at peace under the care of their new-found Saviour. At midnight the church drums were beaten and we assembled again for a few minutes for a Watch Night service of prayer and praise as the New Year came in, a fitting end to a time that was to many the beginning of new life.

One result of this convention was the offer of 12 enthusiastic volunteers to go to Shyira and 8 for Kigeme. Another important result was a deeper oneness and fellowship between the missionaries and the born-again Africans. Bill Church, for one, wrote of his own tendency to be reserved and stand-offish with the African hospital staff: 'These and several other things hinder us, and me especially. I am painfully conscious that I ought to be far closer to the *Banyaruanda* [all the people of Ruanda – Bahutu, Batutsi and Batwa] than I am.' And as Joe commented, 'My brother had touched on what became the greatest fruit of the Revival, deep oneness and fellowship with the Africans. We found that when once we had repented and in some cases asked forgiveness for our prejudice and white superiority, a new realm in relationships was entered into which altered the character of all our work.'

Joe extended this wish for openness in other relationships too, and began to discuss deeper personal and spiritual issues with his father in his letters home. At Gahini the *Abaka*, 'those on fire', talked enthusiastically about the Lord and His salvation. Some responded, but others, particularly the older church teachers, took offence, so that along with the new deep unity between the *Abaka*, division between them and others could also be felt. As Joe recognized, the Devil was eager to spoil God's good work, but 'after much prayer, God gave the victory'. Whereas previously hours used to be spent settling squabbles ('hearing words'), now there were hardly any. With Bill Church, who had been away doing stints at Shyira and Kigeme, now back and able to help with the rapidly growing medical work at Gahini, Joe and his team of hospital workers and teachers undertook a series of medical and evangelistic safaris throughout 1934 covering hundreds of miles of eastern Ruanda, teaching and healing from morning till night. As they worked closely together, Joe realized later that 'Unknown to us, God was preparing a team to take the message of revival to Uganda.'

But first came the long-awaited movement into Urundi. At last the two new sites for which the Mission had applied – Buhiga and Matana – were officially granted. Bill Church was chosen to work at Buhiga and Kosiya Shalita at Matana. On 27 December 1934 the great safari, a journey of 150 miles all done on foot as there were no roads south after Kibungu, moved off amid great rejoicing. As always, Joe described it well:

Perhaps this was one of the last big safaris in this part of Africa because head porterage is rightly now forbidden wherever a vehicle can be used. We read about the little army of Jehoshaphat (2 Chron. 20:12) that rose up early in the morning and went into battle singing and praising. My brother Bill was moving about in his room before it was light, and from the early hours onwards the seventy Ruanda porters began to assemble outside. Many of them had been chosen from our own readers and Christians and they literally did go over the border into Urundi singing with their loads on their heads. It was the first time that 'Jesus loves me' and 'There is a happy land' had pierced the silence of those Urundi hills and valleys . . . There were also thirty readers and Christians who had volunteered to preach and start new churches in Urundi.

Things were going to be far from easy for Bill. A Roman Catholic priest took up residence on the same hill in order to warn people against the new teaching. Rumours were circulated that Bill was like a wild beast who would devour them. He was ill with malaria and alone – nicknamed *le solitaire* by local Belgian officials. He wrote:

Pioneer work sounds most thrilling in England, but I find it rather damp. As I write, rain pours steadily on to my tent and in a storm I have to support it. Pioneer work means starting from scratch on an expanse of wet grass, in a congested tent. Cooking is done in an ant-hole, medical work out of soap-boxes. Instead of a large crowd of friendly Christians, there is a crowd of pagan strangers, and thieves come nearly every night. Please don't think I'm complaining. On the contrary, I'm enjoying a new experience. I believe this is where God would have me serve Him and that is all that matters.

A year later Bill had achieved a lot medically, and people were thronging to the church although not one was truly 'born again'. He acknowledged gratefully the help of the Spirit-filled Christians from Gahini who were working with him. Things were far from easy either for Kosiya Shalita on his piercingly cold plateau at Matana, but he started a wonderful work, which was later developed by Dr and Mrs Sharp and the Guillebauds. All were greatly encouraged by the fact that in Urundi there was to be close co-operation with other small missions – Danish Baptists, Canadian Free Methodists and American Friends who linked with them to form an Alliance of Protestant Missions working in the area.

One person at Gahini who grew greatly in spiritual stature at this time was Blasio Kigozi, the younger brother of Simeon Nsibambi of Kampala. Simeon had led his young brother to Christ, and saw him as his 'first fruit in Jesus'. Conscious that God had a calling for him outside Uganda, Blasio had responded way back in 1929 to a call to go to teach in the school at Gahini. He worked there with Cecil Verity, and then went back to Uganda to train for ordination, returning to Gahini as an ordained deacon in 1934 to open a new evangelists' training school in January 1935. It did not start well. The students resented Blasio's enthusiasm, and eventually six of them walked out, leaving Blasio feeling totally defeated. He retired into a little *kazu* or prayer hut he had built, and stayed there for two weeks, rarely emerging and eating very little. During that week the Lord met him in a new way, and from then onwards he continued his ministry with new power. He radiated the love and the spirit of Jesus and wherever he went people were convicted of sin and drawn to Christ. He, Joe and Yosiya Kinuka developed a close friendship and spiritual unity, spending hours together praying and studying the Bible. Blasio in particular was gripped with a new sense of urgency. He seemed almost to be burning himself out, but God had important things for him to do.

12

1935–1938: Revival in Uganda

In 1935, Joe was still feeling 'sometimes like a dog straining at the leash'. On 3 September he wrote in his private journal, 'For years I have felt an urge to take a band of three or four real soul-winners for missions but we are waiting for God to open the way.' He was aware of the danger, like his dog Jasper in the bush, of tearing past the trail and losing it and coming back cut and tired: 'I must learn to go slow with Him and "wait on the Lord".' He couldn't know it then, but God's call was to come just four days later.

The spiritual battle was continuing at Gahini. Apart from the growing 'keen crowd', Joe himself felt misunderstood and isolated. Some of the missionaries opposed him. Others, including his brother Bill at this stage, were certainly not wholly with him, and neither was Kosiya Shalita. As Joe wrote, 'I often pray now, "How long, O Lord, how long?" I sometimes feel I cannot stick it much longer.' One constant criticism was that the hospital was interfering in the church work. As Joe saw it, 'That word interference is blown round the hill by an evil spirit.' In particular, Blasio Kigozi's tireless preaching of the need to repent and to turn to Christ for forgiveness aroused the anger of the teachers and lay readers of the village churches round about. 'There is too much preaching about sin,' they wrote. 'We are baptized and confirmed Christians of several years' standing.

Isn't that enough? Do *we* need to be born again? Is it right for a student to suggest that a schoolmaster is drinking or committing adultery?' But the Holy Spirit continued his gracious work, Blasio and the others continued to pray, and slowly people's lives were changed. More and more they turned to their Bibles, eagerly spreading the Good News to others.

There was similar opposition to teaching about the need to be 'born again' in Kabale. Lawrence Barham was deeply concerned about the spiritual situation there, where people tended to think that if they could read they were Christians, but he was also hopeful that the long-prayed-for revival was in sight. The witness of Kosiya Nkundiye, who had previously been the Barhams' cook and who took a holiday from Gahini to testify to his old friends in Kabale, together with a letter from Blasio telling of his new infilling of the Holy Spirit, led Lawrence to write to Joe at the beginning of September 1935 inviting him to come with a band of workers to lead a special Convention for lay evangelists and teachers at Kabale. On Friday 6 September, the night before the letter arrived, God spoke to Joe through a vivid dream in which he and a colleague at Bart's Hospital made up a quarrel and forgave each other with tears. As Joe described, 'I lay awake and realized that for a long time I had not been forgiving people properly and had been remembering unkind things they said which brought a barrier of fear and dislike of them. I determined to act on this in the future with God's help. At breakfast, "like a bolt from the blue", there on the table lay Lawrence's letter inviting us to Kabale in three weeks' time. I realized that the dream was sent by God to prepare me for this call.'

The Christians at Gahini were being welded into a team and had been ready for some time for such a call as this. The Convention was to be from Sunday 22 to Monday 30 September. Simeon Nsibambi and a friend from Kampala

Burrough Green Rectory. The family home for twenty-one years, 1895–January 1917.

The family, with pets, at Burrough Green 1916.

At one of the "jumps" at Bovington Camp, with the Tank Corps 1919.

Joe in Tank Corps uniform 1919.

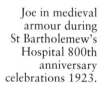

Joe in medieval armour during St Bartholemew's Hospital 800th anniversary celebrations 1923.

Norfolk Broads V.P.S.C. "Walrus" cruise April 1925. Joe and brother Bill in V-necked pullovers sitting on deck.

left Joe with flag and ship's bell presented to him at the 50th anniversary celebration of the Walrus cruises, April 1974.

right Sons John, David, Robin and Michael and grandsons Jonathan, Martin, Simon and Mark and granddaughter Amanda on the Broads during the 50th anniversary celebrations.

Mount Sabinio, Rwanda, 12,000 ft. Ascended by Joe, January 1934.

Joe with his new box-body car, 1930.

Joe Church and Decima Tracey at the time of their engagement.

Joe and Decima's wedding reception at Dr and Mrs Albert Cook's house,
Kampala, Uganda, 1930, with Decima's sister Vera, Dr Leonard Sharp
(holding Alsatian 'Jasper'), and the Cooks.

Joe with Jasper enjoying the view from the veranda of the doctor's house, Gahini 1936.

Decima giving sewing lessons on the veranda, Gahini.

Rain clouds over Lake Mohasi. View from the doctor's house.

John and David running naked in a tropical rainstorm, Gahini 1936.

Yosiya Kinuka and Joe speaking to famine patients at Gahini
Hospital 1929.

The lakeside retreat where Joe kept his boats, and planted trees.

left Rev (later Bishop) Kosiya Shalita and family.

above Simeon Nsibambi.

Rev Yosiya and Dorakasi Kinuka on his new motorbike, Gahini 1951.

Christmas Day sports at Gahini 1933. Hospital staff competing in the high jump and archery.

left Kamondo, Tutsi chieftness. Supporter during the famine, 1929.
right Tutsi gentlemen's hairdresser, creating the masunzu hairstyle.

Joe and Decima at King Musinga's court, Ruanda 1931.

Top Section of the congregation at the Kabale Convention 1955.

left William Nagenda and Joe on arrival in India May 1952.

above Joe and Festo Kivengere greeting evangelist Billy Graham on his arrival in Urundi 1960.

Kabale convention team 1955.

The first team to Kenya, Kabete 1937. Obadiah Kariuki (later Bishop), Joe, brother Howard, Livingstone Kiarii, Francis Kaboyo, Biangwa (with autoharp), Erinesti Nabugabo, Simeon Nsibambi and Paulo Gahundi. (Seven languages with one message.)

The first Kabale preparatory school, in the doctor's garage 1938. Eileen Faber, with John Sharp and John, David and Robin Church.

Kabale Preparatory School at the entrance to the new building in 1945. Steadily growing to over 200 Ugandan children after the country's independence.

Gahini Hospital during construction, 1951.

Kabarole Hospital, Fort Portal, Uganda. Opening ceremony 18 March 1965, with Princess Margaret and Lord Snowdon, the Omukama and Princess Ada of Toro, the Archbishop of Uganda Erica Sabiti, Joe, Decima, David and Robin Church.

The Church family together at Decima's sister's house in Devon, 1952. Joe, Decima, John, David, Robin, Michael and Janine.

joined several leading Christians from Ruanda on the team, which was led by Joe, Yosiya and Blasio. The Convention started as planned on the Sunday with two days of quiet preparation for the team, then, as a cold mountain mist blew through the open windows of the big Kabale church on the Tuesday morning, the talks began. Subjects covered included sin, repentance, the new birth, separation from the world, the Holy Spirit and the victorious life – one topic each day, based on readings from the Scofield Reference Bible – and the Convention ended with a praise meeting on the Sunday. Joe described the strategy in one of his regular letters to the Cambridge University Missionary Band, as follows:

> The main feature of the Bible team form of mission, as we are evolving it, is to have a convention on Keswick lines, i.e good old fashioned Bible readings on the deepening of the spiritual life as the main feature. People come with notebooks and pencils and the day begins with a blackboard Bible reading on the subject for the day. The team go as personal workers and for prayer support, and can be called upon to speak. At Kabale they lodged out all over the station, and in this way the subject for the day is carried into the native surroundings, and is talked out into the night – and the night, as it was with Nicodemus, is the time the East does spiritual business. They don't like sermons. Bands of workers, soul-winners, going out like this, backed and prepared by prayer and using the Bible as their power and authority, is to my mind a scheme worth developing . . . so the thing grows.

One interested young participant was later to play a leading role in the Christian Church worldwide. Festo Kivengere, grandson of King Makobore of the Bahororo tribe, had left his home village to attend Kigezi High School, the Ruanda Mission School in Kabale. Commenting years later on the meetings, he observed that what was special was not so much what they said – those were the basic gospel truths – but, 'There was power in what they said. We hadn't seen that before . . . our attention was riveted by the shining faces of these men who obviously had spiritual freedom, were in love with God, and at peace with one another. We listened, wide-eyed, to what they had to say.' For Festo it was to be some years before he was to find the joy of salvation himself; many more years before he was to become Bishop of Kigezi and an internationally known preacher and evangelist. For the moment, as people slipped quietly home after the meetings, he observed, 'It was too new and startling for most people. Yet we felt strangely restless, strangely stirred.' Soon the effects began to be more dramatic, and Festo began to hear strange stories: 'Within a month, people began to weep unexpectedly, dream dreams of heaven, or cry out under conviction.' Many found forgiveness at the cross of Christ, and with it great joy. As one young missionary wrote, 'Christians are now on fire. Many have been convicted of secret sins, returning money stolen years ago . . . God seems to have been using dreams to convict people.' And as Lawrence Barham described, 'Preaching bands have gone out all through the district and many are stirred.' There was naturally opposition as well.

There were difficulties too when the team got back to Gahini. The revival was still meeting opposition even from among the missionaries: the headmistress of the girls' school expelled some girls for going out at night without permission to a prayer meeting in the church; and the hospital sister was deeply upset because not content with being away himself, Joe had insisted on taking Yosiya away from the hospital without her agreement, to go to Kabale for the Convention. It was a question of priorities. To Joe the spiritual work with people was of prime importance; to those trying to run a school or a hospital, it could make things difficult. As when some years later Nurse Beatrice Louis found herself getting very uptight on operating days as Joe would frequently be late. Eventually he would come in beaming: 'I've just had such a lovely chat with Tomasi [the gardener].' 'But Joe, we are waiting to operate', she would protest.

In fact, for the moment it seemed that it might be possible for Joe to be released for full-time evangelistic work. Archdeacon Pitt Pitts of the CMS, now Field Secretary to the Ruanda Mission, was living at Gahini for a while. As Joe described, 'At the end of one of our times of prayer in his house he called me aside and said, "I have a very important question to put to you, Joe, one that may affect all the rest of your life." ' The suggestion was that Joe should give up medical work and concentrate full-time on mission and evangelism. Talking it over with the Archdeacon, in Joe's words:

I stressed that an evangelist should ideally to my mind be a man who is in a job, who works out his message in the rough and tumble of life in what we now call 'God's revival school', but who is foot-loose enough to be able to slip off from time to time when calls come. I said that I thought that very few are called to be full-time evangelists. Preaching and healing have always gone hand in hand in God's work. I enjoyed my surgical operations and watching my patients get well; and there seemed to be no place for a whole-time evangelist who was a layman in the Anglican set-up. Also I was often told that I had no preaching voice and that people could not hear me well. And added to all this, our evangelistic teams had always grown up out of men and women in their jobs on a busy mission station. We knew nothing of 'lone-wolfing'. I was torn between two choices. My call to evangelism was so strong that I knew it would entail my not being able to keep up my medicine. God had over-ruled in this in giving me a wife better qualified medically than I, who kept up with medical literature over the years, but at that time she was fully occupied with the running of the household and the bringing up of our energetic boys, as well as with the careful keeping of the hospital and family accounts. So after much prayer and heart-searching I asked that I might continue with part-time medical work.

It was the start of a change of direction, which was to lead to an important move for Joe and his family in a few years' time. Meanwhile there were fresh challenges. Ten days before Christmas, at the end of 1935, Decie and four-year-old John went down with a severe attack of malaria but, having given them a new anti-malarial injection, Joe had reluctantly to leave them and drive to Mbarara in Uganda for supplies and spare parts for the car. Delays in repairing the car found Joe frustrated and still at Mbarara on Christmas Eve, facing being away from his sick family and all the special events at Gahini for Christmas and, in addition, being stuck with the missionaries at Mbarara who were not in sympathy with the revival. He was thinking of getting away on his own for the day, as the needed spare part still had not come, when the Holy Spirit made it clear that he must apologize to Mr Clark, the missionary, for his negative thoughts and ask to stay and spend Christmas with them. At once he was not only welcomed, but invited to preach at the main Christmas service in the morning. Then, giving Joe only a second to decide before introducing him as the preacher, Mr Clark leaned across and asked if he could announce that Joe, Blasio and Yosiya would conduct a week of prayer for clergy and evangelists at Mbarara in ten days' time. What could Joe do but say 'yes'.

Back at Gahini he found Decie still very ill but soon to recover. But when next morning he told Yosiya and Blasio of the invitation to Mbarara, Blasio remained unusually silent. His wife and family were waiting for him in Kampala where they had gone on ahead for Christmas. How could he disappoint them? He himself was exhausted and very much in need of a rest. Then, as Joe described, 'Yosiya said quietly, "Blasio, this may be the last work that God has given you to do. Let us go." That was enough. We were soon praising and planning and praying, but what prophetic words they proved to be as Blasio prepared for his last journey to Kampala.'

Joe himself could not stay away from the hospital again so soon, so he drove Yosiya and Blasio to the Uganda border where Mr Clark met them and took them on. 'So we parted,' wrote Joe. 'I left them there to run their first mission alone.' Little did Joe know that he was saying goodbye to Blasio for the last time as he waved them off. The special week began at Mbarara, following the same teaching plan as at Kabale except that Blasio had asked for one extra subject to be included – judgement, or the wrath to come. Oblivious to his own need for rest, and almost as if he had a premonition that he did not have long to serve his Master, he was up all night twice that week pleading with people to be saved. Perhaps he was bitten by the dreaded ticks of Relapsing Fever then. Shortly afterwards he was admitted to Mengo Hospital with a very high temperature, and on 25 January he died and went to be with his Lord. He was buried on the cathedral hill at Namirembe, and on his gravestone near the cathedral's east window was inscribed the one Luganda word, *Zuzuka*! – 'Awake!'

Meanwhile, back at Gahini and unaware of what had happened, Joe was feeling defeated by difficulties and overwork. On Sunday 26 he set out alone, on his bicycle, to have a quiet day at his special spot in the game country, reading the Bible and praying. The following Friday evening news of Blasio's death reached Gahini by runner just as everyone was going up to the big schoolroom for the weekly prayer meeting. His loss was a heavy blow. To Joe he had become not only a close personal friend but also a valued colleague: 'He was almost daily in and out of my house. I almost hear his cheery laugh. He had grown to be a man of God and was one of the deepest friends I've ever had.' But Blasio had insisted as he was dying that 'There must be no tears', and the Holy Spirit told Joe the same thing: 'My Bible opened at that strange passage of the Prophet Ezekiel, chapter 24, verses 15–18, where the prophet was told to carry on as before even after deep personal bereavement: "Behold I take away from thee the desire of thine eyes with a stroke: yet shalt thou neither mourn nor weep." (That night the prophet's wife died.) So we carried on as we knew Blasio would have wished. Later that night the strains of "Onward, Christian Soldiers" came echoing through the station from the Bible School.' Joe wrote the story of Blasio's life, *Awake, Uganda!* and, based on his manuscript, the Church Missionary Society published a booklet called *Awake! An African Calling. The Story of Blasio Kigozi and His Vision of Revival.*

Among the many people who were profoundly affected by Blasio's death was his friend and near relation, William Nagenda, son of a Muganda landowner and a government clerk in Uganda. As Joe wrote, 'He was a truly saved man but he did not have the vision and zeal of his brother-in-law – until Blasio died. He immediately offered to the Bishop of Uganda to go to Ruanda where Blasio had served. He was unknown to any of us, but when we were asked by the Bishop which station would like to have him, my hand went up because I knew that he was a convert of Nsibambi. God was answering our prayers for one to take Blasio's place.'

Sophisticated and well educated, fluent in English, self-confident and at ease with Europeans, William joined the team at Gahini, and a happy and fruitful partnership between him and Joe began. Despite sadness and difficulties, 1936 was a productive year. In March, Joe completed the book of Bible studies based on the Scofield Reference Bible, which he had been working on for the previous seven years. Entitled *Every Man a Bible Student*, it consisted of over 40 simple studies – mainly a list of references following a subject right through the Bible – on key gospel themes: God, Man, Sin, Christ, Repentance, Salvation, and so on. These were the Bible themes which Joe and Yosiya had expounded to the crowds at the hospital at Gahini – the way Joe worked out for letting the Bible speak, as their language and skill in exposition were so limited. One of the themes, on the Holy Spirit, was the study that had thrilled the hearts of Joe and Simeon Nsibambi back in 1929 and given them the first taste of revival. Although criticized by some as being theologically weak – and Joe, it must be remembered, was not theologically trained – the book was used by student Christian Unions and other groups all over the world, reprinted 17 times, and brought out in several subsequent editions and in many different languages.

In June Joe and a team led a mission at the Bishop Tucker Memorial College, Mukono, Uganda, in response to an invitation from Bishop Stuart, successor to Bishop Willis. But before they went, remarkable things were happening. In May, ecstatic signs began to appear in village churches near Gahini, rather like those at Kabale. There was much conviction of sin, accompanied by violent weeping and shaking. In one or two cases, women became dumb. The revival and its unexpected effects were still causing division in the Mission. Even Joe was puzzled. Trying to understand the outward manifestations which were accompanying the people's repentance and faith, Joe wrote, 'It seemed evident that there are depths in the subconscious that can surge up in strange and unusual manifestations when the Holy Spirit is stirring people and convicting of sin . . .' Joe and Dr Algie Stanley Smith spent a quiet day together praying and studying what the Bible had to say. Joe concluded that whereas the outward signs might or might not occur, 'Revival is *repentance* and a daily coming back to the Cross with a broken and contrite heart. Therefore it must be obligatory . . . Seeing this gave us great assurance (and some felt intransigence) in those days. But it was to us the very key to unloosing God's power in all our work.'

On 8 June, as Cecil Verity and Joe were saying goodbye to students of the evangelists' training school who were leaving for the holidays, Cecil made a public confession of failure to Joe who felt impelled to reciprocate, saying that he had allowed wrong thoughts and lack of love to hinder his working with him. Then confessions and testimonies began among the students and went on the whole morning. As Joe read chapter 21 of John's Gospel, 'Feed my sheep', 18 students stood up and volunteered to spend their holidays preaching all over East Africa without pay. The next day, Joe and the team set off for Mukono, via Kabale and Mbarara. At a gathering in Mbarara church something happened which Joe had never experienced before: 'A man began to cry out and howl at the top of his voice. I was alarmed and made the people sit down. The man continued weeping lying on the floor . . . I called him up to the chancel to say what he had experienced. He was one of the most trusted Christians, a government interpreter. He stood beside me weeping and in halting words gave a moving testimony. He said that he had seen a vision of Christ in the church and he saw the awful state of the lost and was overwhelmed with grief for his own past.'

A quiet weekend of preparation for the team, when 12 Africans and 4 Europeans gathered in the Bishop's hilltop house overlooking Kampala, ended with a service in the cathedral when the Archdeacon held up a copy of the life of Blasio (who was to have been part of the team), *Awake, Uganda!*, and appealed to the Church of Uganda to awake from its sleep. Then came the week of the mission. It had been intended as a preparatory mission at the theological college at Mukono for a series of wider missions which the Bishop was planning for 1937 and in which he hoped the students would be involved. As Kevin Ward described it (*Obedient Rebels*, p. 200), 'The mission was fraught with misunderstandings. J.S. Herbert [veteran missionary and at that time warden of the college] felt that he had not been consulted and responded negatively both to the message and to the style of these over-enthusiastic, over-confident young Africans and missionaries . . . the theological tutor, J.C. Jones, also had strong reservations about the emotionalism of it all.'

But Joe and his team were greatly encouraged as some 40 people turned wholeheartedly to Christ, several of them the better educated among the students. As Joe realized, these decisions for Christ among theological students posed a vital question: were these people saved before, and were they now just revived, or were they never really born again? All seemed convinced that they had only had a nominal Christianity before. Also, to quote Kevin Ward again, 'Joe Church left Mukono convinced that one of the most intractable problems the revival had to contend with in the church was "clericalism" – *obukulu* in Luganda – and that Mukono was the chief propagator of the obukulu mentality, with its excessive exaltation of the clerical office, its undue deference to authority and its stifling of the spirit of revival' (*Obedient Rebels*, p. 200).

Although no one foresaw it at the time, this influx of new spiritual life at the college was to have dramatic repercussions. Joe had sent a *Call to Prayer* pamphlet back to England asking urgently for prayer just before the mission and, as they drove off in their cars, cheered on by a crowd of students singing mission hymns and choruses, the team were very conscious that many had been praying and that their prayers had been answered.

Next came a family holiday at Kisenyi on Lake Kivu. Kisenyi, 'place of sand', gave them several wonderful holidays over the years, camping, swimming, trekking up the slopes of the Bufumbira mountains. Joe and Decie got back to Gahini in July to find that amazing things had been happening in their absence – manifestations of the work of God's Spirit which Joe also ascribed to the great volume of prayer which had gone up.

As well as dreams, visions and people falling down in trances, many were claiming to have entered a new life and to be following Christ. But although he had not been there, even Joe described what happened in the girls' school as really alarming when, starting with four girls praying and weeping out loud, more and more girls were convicted of their sin and began weeping and confessing until the room was in pandemonium. The missionaries tried to deal with it and it went on for three days, with women who had come in for evening classes also collapsing and having to be helped home to bed, where they often remained prostrate for hours. Miss Skipper, the headmistress, who had been very wary of emotionalism and hysteria, herself became convinced by the calm and peaceful trust in Jesus that these girls and women displayed when eventually they emerged from what appeared to be a hysterical state. As Cecil Verity wrote, 'A spirit of awe seems to be over the place.' Over a thousand people packed the church on 26 July on what Joe described as 'one of the most wonderful days at Gahini'.

There was a lot of noise, too, as people began singing hymns all night, syncopating the tunes to the African six/eight time. Some found this too much to bear as they had work to do next day; but Joe rejoiced that instead of heathen drums and clapping resounding through the night at harvest time, the hillside was resounding with praises to God. He felt that rather than 'the usual missionary method, the heavy hand of the white man coming down in school-masterly fashion', it was better to pray and advise and get the trust of the African, and to leave it to God to show him what was right. Rosemary Guillebaud commented years later on this: 'The endless hymn singing, often with drumming, meant lack of sleep, plus anger and annoyance, for those of us not in the fellowship, but I think I viewed that part of it differently when I "came into blessing".'

Already there was awareness of the dangers of counterfeit and of confusing the manifestations with the deeper reality. A small schoolgirl confessed to Miss Skipper that she had put saliva round her eyes to look as though she had been weeping. And when an imposing Christian leader began to weep and shake in his prayer, the feeling began to get around that unless you did these things you weren't really filled with the Spirit. It was a difficult time, with the Roman Catholics accusing the Mission of encouraging Devil worship and the pagans saying that the *muzungu* (white man) had bewitched them. Joe and the others rejoiced that God's Spirit was at work, and continued to encourage a genuine response to the faithful teaching of God's word. Two of the most lasting and genuine marks of the revival were deepening fellowship across all tribal, social and racial barriers, expressed in fellowship meetings when experiences of God and confessions were shared informally and at a deep level; and 'walking in the light', based on 1 John 1:7 – a transparent sincerity between believers. Encouraged by the tremendous effect of their *Call to Prayer* pamphlet, Joe wrote and circulated a three-page leaflet called *Victorious Praying*, to mobilize revival prayer fellowships throughout the world, of which many thousands were printed and used.

In 1937 the team travelled widely, taking missions in different places in Uganda, and then at the beginning of April, as Joe and Decie left Gahini and headed home for leave in

England, they were invited by Joe's brother, Howard, now posted there with the CMS, and his wife Lizzo to hold a week's mission at Kabete, one of the main CMS stations in Kenya. This was the first visit of a revival team to Kenya.

Back in England, their two families at Willand and Fen Ditton were waiting for them, with grandparents delighted to welcome not only John and David, but Robin, born in January 1935. Joe as always became quickly involved in travelling, finding 'a great welcome from the CICCU. One entered the Henry Martyn Hall with the feeling that here was the power-house that had loosed God's movings in Ruanda and Uganda.' As he travelled the country and spent time at the Keswick Convention as chaplain to the group of Cambridge students there, he found many people concerned and praying for revival. It was at Keswick too that Joe conceived the idea of the 'Uganda Seven', based on the Cambridge Seven who went to China in 1885. The call was for seven young men 'of Keswick outlook' to go out to Uganda to help with teaching and follow-up in centres where revival missions had been held, and in the event three went: Bill Butler, Philip Ridsdale and Dr Charles Sergel.

In March 1938, Joe sailed ahead of his family back to Africa but this time to Kabale, Uganda, where he was to build their new home and to concentrate on his evangelistic work and begin to implement the plan for the Uganda Seven. In fact, after a frustrating time of uncertainty, it turned out that he didn't have to build a house after all – Archdeacon Pitt Pitts moved to the Ruanda Mission's central station in Ibuye, and his house at Kabale became the Church family home for the next eight years. Joe concentrated on evangelistic work, and especially on key Christian gatherings and plans for missions in Kenya. Amid increasing rumblings of war in Europe and rumblings too of opposition to the revival, Joe pushed ahead in the spiritual battle while looking forward to being reunited with his family. It was a hard time, and he missed Decie, writing in his private diary, 'I live over again the times when we two have walked with Him, and I drop off to sleep feeling her in my arms again – only to wake to another cool Kabale morning when my dreams blow away like the early mountain mists.'

13

1938–1944: Kabale, a Children's Paradise

In September 1938, war hung in the balance. Germany was threatening to invade Czechoslovakia. The British fleet was mobilized. Decie and the three boys, John, David and Robin, aged 7, 6 and 3 were on a German ship the *Adolph Woermann*, off Italian Eritrea in the Red Sea. With them was a friend of Decie's family, Miss Eileen Faber, who had offered to help as governess to the children. Anxious for their safety, Joe cabled Decie's older brother, Christopher Tracey, who was then Acting Governor of the Sudan, in Khartoum, asking him to take action if there was any danger of their being interned. Christopher acted at once to get them off the ship and, instead of following the Red Sea and east coast route to Mombasa, they headed west across the desert by train to Khartoum. From here a steamship took them up the Nile to Juba near the Uganda border. For Joe, who had been involved in big Christian gatherings in Kenya, 'it was a big test to see the German boat steam into Mombasa without my family on board – but God over-ruled. I set off to drive 1,500 miles to Juba in the Sudan to meet them.'

As always, nothing was wasted in Joe's life or in God's economy, and he visited several mission stations on the way. 'Then, at Juba, the hottest place I had yet struck in Africa, I ran out of petrol in the main street, right in front of the CMS bookshop. Inside I met Willoughby Carey, the Secretary of CMS Sudan, who at once told me he had been wanting to see me about the strange happenings of revival that were going on in southern Sudan. So I saw another reason why God had sent me on this long journey.'

The next day, 'I got up very early and from the top of some large granite boulders above the still sleeping town of Juba I watched the sun rise slowly through the grey mists of the Sudan papyrus "sudd" which stretched out for miles and miles to the north. I could distinctly see a little wisp of black smoke rising from the funnel of the boat as it wound its way slowly up the silver thread of the Nile. At 9 a.m. she rounded the last bend a few hundred yards from the quay and I could see three pale but terribly excited little boys

waving to me, with their mother! (They had nearly died of dysentery on the way.) Six hundred miles more, in easy stages, brought us on Friday, 28 October, to the green mown lawns and English flowers of our new home at Kabale in Uganda, and their seven weeks' voyage was ended.'

Now began a time of exceptional happiness for the three boys. Already for them Africa was home, evoked by the lemony scent of the pepper trees, the songs of the birds and by a hundred other scents and sounds. Here at Kabale the family was to live in the rambling mission house vacated by Archdeacon Pitt Pitts who had moved to Urundi. Joe had been working with his usual energy to make the place ready for them, planning, improving and planting to create an earthly paradise. Even higher above sea level than Ruanda, the climate is relatively cool in the Kigezi hills. Mist collects in the evening and breaks up with the rising sun in the morning, so the hills are always green and fresh. It was this cool climate which led to Joe's enthusiasm for fireplaces. To make a home, you had to have a hearth. He acquired a book on the subject, and had soon made a fire which not only didn't smoke, but also looked beautiful, with inglenook seats and other 'humanizing touches' – so much so, that other missionaries were soon asking his help to do the same.

Blissfully unaware of the spiritual difficulties their father often faced, the boys lived out of doors, climbing trees, building tree houses. To David, remembering it later, it seemed that they inhabited a little island on the mission hill. It was rather like being on a great liner at sea – isolated, yet with loving people around them, protected, secure. A year later in November 1939, a fourth son, Michael, was born. And it was he, troubled later by the separations which older missionary children so often endured in those days, who many years after dug most deeply back into this time as he sought to rediscover its happiness – 'a resource to fall back on in the bleak times that followed'. Thinking back into his childhood self, he remembered how 'pets are very important in our home. We have little cairn terrier dogs and cats and lots of rabbits.' As he recalled too, 'I am surrounded by black people, who work in our home, cooking, helping in the house and garden and looking after us children (especially Margareta Kabageni, my *ayah*, who looks after, loves and cares for me). Almost all the people around us are black except for the missionaries, government officials and their children. The people around are called Bachiga and they speak Luchiga, which I don't understand very well. They are always very kind to me and I love them very much. They tell me stories and show me how to do all sorts of exciting things like making fires and bows and arrows.'

Most important of all, the family was together, so that as Michael wrote much later: 'Once upon a time, when I was five years old, I often felt joyful . . . I remember clearly a family holiday we had on Lake Bunyoni – a few miles across the Kigezi hills from our home in Kabale and on an island called Bufundi. Our whole family are together.' He saw himself as 'big head, thin legs always running to try and keep up with big brothers. When I was five, John and David were already teenagers and had a special connection with Dad – they built our sailing boat *The Spray* together, and the model of the yacht *Shamrock* which I remember well.' And of the holiday,

> I remember a bungalow and overflow tent on Bufundi Island and a wooden pier where we moored *The Spray* and held the famous water fight one misty early morning with the Sharps – the family on the other island. It all has a very *Swallows and Amazons* feel about it which was to be repeated many times on the Norfolk Broads after that. I remember hot sun and lying in the boat listening to the lapping of the water. I remember sailing races round 'Prisoners' Island' – we won of course – and I remember purple water-lilies and fishing and magical views of Muhavura and bonfires.

From these holiday memories, an important aspect of Joe's character emerges. Michael highlighted two contrasting images of his father: 'Holy Joe the missionary – serious, intense, doctor, preacher, pioneer, dutiful father, public Joe; the other the relaxed playful sailor, wild man and fun.' The latter has already begun to emerge in Joe's love of sports and sailing as a young man; and particularly in his joy in sharing these enthusiasms with other youngsters in the Walrus cruises. Here in Kabale, as he wrote, 'I take the boys out once a week exploring. Today we have been rock-climbing, even with Robin aged five.' Already at Gahini too, before they moved to Kabale, Joe had made a bathing place down by the lake, under a big spreading acacia tree which he had planted, and a pier made from a single giant eucalyptus trunk split by patient wedging. He and the boys loved making things. David made a canoe, patiently covering its surface with papier mâché made from hundreds of old *British Medical Journals*, and finishing it with fabric and tar.

Michael became absorbed in model-making, which as he wrote later was to provide a vital survival strategy for him at boarding school as he withdrew to quiet activity in the little model room behind the clock up under the eaves at St Lawrence College.

A few years later, in 1944, when he was working again part of the time at Gahini, Joe wrote a poem about the huge acacia by the lake. He called it simply 'My Tree'.

Gahini's a life-sized picture,
    the canvas was sun-baked clay
Which once was barren and treeless
    for thousands of years, they say.

Then I painted it with trees and with flowers,
    I've walked on the roads I have made.
I've planted it with tiny seeds
    that God has turned into shade.

Now my picture's alive and quivering,
    sparkling with silver and dew,
Sunbirds sucking and singing
    midst flowers of every hue.

Jesus now lives in my picture
    as he walked in Galilee,
He sits by the beds with my patients,
    but he loves the shade of my tree.

At other times, 'We would go hunting out in the game country behind Gahini, a tremendous thrill for the African schoolboys. The women would prepare food and collect wild flowers or watch birds while the men in their oldest clothes would go hunting for an oribi or bush buck or occasionally a hartebeest. Then if there was time, we would cook meat on sticks round a camp fire . . .'

Of course there were troubles. One Easter morning Michael and two cousins – Howard's sons – rebelling against being constantly called 'titches' by the older boys, made their feelings 'clear as mud'. A good rainstorm provided a huge puddle, so they smeared mud all over John and David's room, beds, games and puzzles and all. Then in horror at what they had done the shamefaced little group ran off down the hill into Kabale, only to be dragged back and given the one and only beating Michael ever received – Joe, like his father, was against any sort of corporal punishment. Even worse was their banishment from a much-awaited Easter tea party, so that Michael's cries of 'I'll get thinner and thinner until I die' became part of the family folklore. But by and large, as he remembers it, 'My life then was very straightforward and fun. The family was together, the war had ended and was far away, and I had not yet been sent away to school.'

So what did happen about school? Already on the ship out, Eileen Faber had begun teaching John, David and Robin. But almost at once in Kabale she found herself starting a school. Dr Stanley Smith's old garage was converted into a schoolroom and the District Commissioner sent his child over each day from the Government Hill to join the Church boys at what later became known as Kabale Preparatory School (KPS). Gradually the school grew as other European children joined, some as boarders. Other teachers, known as 'aunties', joined the staff. Eventually the converted garage became hopelessly small and a big gift from Eileen made possible the building of a new purpose-built school. Joe, who was an architect at heart, was involved with the planning of the new school building with its much-loved special features, the House at Pooh Corner rooms, the porch with its two carved rabbits, the quiet papyrus-lined prayer room upstairs, with its view over the garden to the distant mountains. The staircase handrail was supported by carved wooden rabbits, one standing upright on each step. As Dr Kenneth Buxton remembered, 'Joe's gifts of craftsmanship and ingenuity played a large part in setting the tone and forming the character of the school.' Eileen, talented, young and eager to give of her best, shared his creativity and vision. While Decie was busy supervising cooks, houseboys and gardeners, sorting mail and doing a hundred other essential things, Eileen taught and inspired the children. They loved her. Michael, not born when it began, joined the school some years later. He has strong memories of Miss Faber: 'Eileen was a good teacher and a gifted artist. She put in amazing care to our first Beacon Reader books, which were hand-copied and illustrated with drawings and photos. Eileen also, as my godmother, wrote illustrated story-books for me, like *Michael Alan and the wooden rabbits.*' Later she was to encourage all the children in the love of painting. A piano was acquired, and music became an important part of school life. The school was remarkably progressive, with the children in 'pow-wow' deciding – and therefore keeping – many of the school rules.

To Michael, as to the others, KPS remained his 'best model of learning', and from the rich jumbled tapestry of school and home he picked out many wonderful memories: stories – experience – gardens – beans – Hiawatha – bows and arrows – swings – giant strides – tree houses – the magnificent bougainvillea bush den with its two-storey interior and great secrecy – sand-pits – birthday rituals – prayer room – giant tortoise – Ethiopian picture of St George and the dragon – stories at night – jigger parades (paraffin and pins and skilful hands and blowing cooling breath) – African staff and girls and cooks and garden. He remembered too magic walks – the mist – Crystal Hill and amethyst treasures – valley walk – Government Hill (posh hotel, golf course, official buildings) – fruit trees: avocados, mountain pawpaws, tree tomatoes, custard apples – dewy mornings with dew-drenched chairs at breakfast – morning mist rising and bright sun . . .

The Church children, in this out-of-the-way place, enjoyed for some years an ideal combination of home and school, both happy and secure, with loving parents and teachers, much freedom and a small group of their peers, both boys and girls, with whom to enjoy this freedom. The school went from strength to strength, eventually taking African children and becoming a much-sought-after fee-paying school. Several of Idi Amin's children were to go there, and he would roll up in a helicopter to collect them at the end of term. In the early days the school had made it possible for missionaries to continue their work knowing that their children were in excellent hands. Eileen remembered much happiness: 'the large sand-pit where several children at a time could build their fantasies; the huge see-saw that could take three children at each end; the water-tank that was big enough to swim in . . . but above all, I remember the happy family atmosphere of the school, set in those beautiful surroundings, and thank God that, from the beginning, it was his school, in which he had the pre-eminence. Many of the children gave their hearts to him during that time and have gone on to a life of Christian service.' Joe felt the same about the school, writing in his diary in May 1943, 'I have rarely been more thrilled in my life, as the school began in the beautiful new building. God seemed to pervade the whole place from the start.'

Despite this, Joe was unhappy. Some of his fellow missionaries disapproved of the way he did things and seemed to think that he had stepped out of line in working too closely *with* the Africans. To the Sharps, for instance, the whole idea of having Africans into the house for fellowship was one they couldn't cope with. Their lifestyle, with their pack of aggressive bull terriers, was very different from Joe and Decie's, and they commented unfavourably on Joe's approach. In some quarters he was even banned from preaching. He couldn't understand it – he had given of his very best for this part of Africa, in the hospital work and in his new role as evangelist, and he had created a paradise at Gahini and at Kabale – what had he done wrong? He was unhappy too because Decie did not seem to be totally with him in the revival. Temperamentally she was more reticent than he, and found it hard to share in the very open and extrovert language and ways of the *Balokole* (Saved Ones). As her son David saw it, she was wonderfully loyal but less able to wave her arms about. Going through a time of distress and self-doubt himself, Joe turned on the one who was dearest to him, telling Decie that she had never really shared his vision for Africa. Understandably, Decie became sad and depressed. Suddenly and unexpectedly the family found itself going through a dark and difficult time.

Into the fray stepped Decie's older sister Vera in Nairobi. She decided that Decie needed to get away for a while, that she needed a break from the intense religious pressure surrounding her. Joe's response was to arrange a super holiday for the family, booking them in at a hotel near the beach at Mombasa, something they had never done before, and hiring bikes on which they 'tore about everywhere, every now and again dropping into the sea to keep cool'. It should have been wonderful but, excited though the boys were, they had an uneasy feeling that something was not quite right. It was even less right when Vera managed to persuade Decie to come to her in Nairobi instead, although the understanding was that Decie would join the family soon. Joe stuck to his plan, and he gave the boys a wonderful time in Mombasa, but the whole episode distressed him very much. This is how he described it in his diary:

Felt burdened about family problems, so decided I must get further myself over many little things with Decie. Prayed much and then wrote long and difficult letter. I felt she was still dominated by her sisters like Vera and not really progressive enough – rather wet-blanketing many of my ideas and schemes – never disloyal to me for a moment, not against my plans – we are always one – but just lacking in *joie-de-vivre* for progressive planning and thinking. She changed plans and came down to Mombasa and we had a little honeymoon at the CMS guest house. The boys went back to school. Many things Decie had not realized . . . Much of it was, as I knew, my fault. We made new plans for the future.

So the crisis resolved itself, both Joe and Decie realizing with the help of God's grace where they had been wrong and how they could understand and support each other more. They were to grow closer and closer for the rest of their long lives together. In the meantime, there was work to be done.

14

1938–1946: Revival: High Enthusiasm and Opposition

Since arriving alone at Kabale in 1938, Joe had, as always, been busy. There were many important meetings and conventions: the Kisenyi Missionaries' Conference in July when repentance and revival touched many missionaries; the 'Kenya Keswick Convention' at Limuru in August, when at one extra-late evening meeting, for the first time white Christians sat and listened while African team members spoke; the 'African Keswick' at the Alliance High School, Kikuyu, in September, and other missions in different parts of Kenya. And at Kabale itself, Joe wrote of 1939, 'A new wave of blessing has been seen this year at Kabale and throughout parts of the district.' On the practical level Joe, who loved tidiness and order, was involved in a campaign to 'clean up the mission mile' – the mile-long 'concession' made by the government to the mission, which tended to become a refuge for ne'er-do-wells. Arguing that saved people should have tidier compounds and cleaner, happier homes than others, every homestead was encouraged to plant food, fruit trees and flowers. Some even stopped brewing beer in their homes. There was some opposition, but the District Commissioner was impressed. Similarly, concerned for the many young people hanging around with nothing to do, Joe unearthed a set of hockey sticks bought with some wedding-present money and taught the high-school boys to play, organizing matches with local Indians and the people on Government Hill, games which would be followed by an evangelistic talk.

In 1938 Joe's brother Bill, returning from the Missionary Conference in Kisenyi to Buhiga in Urundi where he was working, realized from the shining faces that greeted him that revival had broken out. As Bill described, 'People sang choruses all night until they had lost their voices by the morning. Confessions of sin at times were very gross and not repeatable in public.' Soon the African revival leaders began tackling Bill and saying that he was not born again. 'They found me hard to know, distant, and suggested I had sins to confess. It was a most humiliating experience for a missionary who had come from afar to heal the sick and preach the gospel . . . I was tempted to be resentful but overcame this temptation. I resolved to be humble, broken of pride and to admit to sins and failures of which I felt convicted.' Certainly he had found true fellowship with the Africans difficult to achieve, writing home that 'Sometimes I begin to wonder if I really understand any of them . . . The barriers of race, economic status and social customs . . . are very real.' With the help of Archdeacon Pitt Pitts, who covered 1,600 miles driving from Kenya and back to answer Bill's *cri de coeur* over this problem, fellowship was soon restored. Bill, less of a charismatic leader than Joe, thorough and thoughtful, was soon to be a supporter of the revival, describing it in 1939 as 'a real work of the Holy Spirit' and adding, 'It has enabled these Africans really to grasp the meaning of conviction of sin, of repentance and confession. Recently many have come to realize the meaning of the Cross as the place of victory. The future is very uncertain, but it is a joy to know that if we suddenly had to leave the country, we would leave behind some who really know

Christ as their Lord and Saviour and would continue to extend His Kingdom.' Although some Africans probably did take advantage of the 'equal footing' provided by the revival to get their own back on the Europeans, Bill later saw their criticism as African protest against missionary paternalism, of which Joe too was being convicted by the Holy Spirit. 'Bossing my African brothers' was how he put it.

In Kigezi, trouble broke out over the wave of hymn singing that often went on late into the night, so that a curfew was imposed ordering all singing to stop at 10 p.m. But as Joe commented, 'Few people had clocks or watches and 6 p.m. was gauged by the sun setting over the horizon, so 10 o'clock was apt to vary! And after all, from time immemorial the night has been the time to sing in Africa . . .' The song which above all became associated with the revival was a rough translation of a Keswick hymn into Luganda: 'Tukutendereza Yesu' ('We praise you Jesus . . .'). This much-loved chorus was sung repeatedly, often with embracing and dancing, when someone repented, accepting the cleansing of the blood of Christ, and so coming into the light. Joe would never discourage this, although as two missionary colleagues remembered, they never saw Joe dancing in this way himself. So popular did it become, sometimes used simply as a greeting, that William Nagenda and other leaders sometimes had to remind people not to sing the song thoughtlessly.

The more the revival spread, bringing with it God's rich blessings, the more it seemed to throw up difficulties and criticism. Even Mabel Ensor, the Irish nurse who had challenged Joe to leave the Anglican church, now denounced the *Balokole* in her usual forthright style: 'A right and proper shame is done away with. The pharisaism and insolence with which they parade their works of repentance are painful. Rudeness, coarseness, bawling outside places of worship, clawing one another as a sign of fellowship, literally bellowing sacred hymns as though it were a drunken carousel, to the great distress of some godly souls who are scoffed at – what is this?' (From Joe Church papers, *New Way* file: Memorandum 'Some plain reasons etc. . . .')

As Joe wrote, 'Fires are always disturbing and sometimes difficult to control.' In March 1939 he and a team visited a church near Kinyansano where 'there was complete confusion. About a thousand people were gathered, sitting inside and outside the building. Many were prostrate, weeping and crying, while others sat quietly waiting. There was so much noise it was impossible to hold the service. Some were beside themselves with grief. In places the floor was wet below their faces and their bodies convulsed with shaking that went on and on, apparently uncontrollably. They had been like this for over an hour.'

Joe's task here was to give biblical teaching on assurance, and gradually peace and joy was seen on many faces and the sound of hymns began to fill the air. One important feature of Joe's leadership of the revival, and of Lawrence Barham's equally, was the way in which manifestations were always carefully checked for their scriptural basis. If people were beginning to wander off onto a wrong path, this would gently be pointed out from the Bible. Always they would be encouraged. Never would the work of the Spirit be quenched.

Missionaries who worked with Joe remembered some revealing things. There were the red flags shaped like sailing boat burgees which he made and put up on the wall with the single word, HIGHEST. As the group prayed before a decision, the important question uppermost was

always, 'What does God want in this situation? What, in this situation, is the HIGHEST?' As a result, Joe could sometimes appear indecisive. He wasn't, but he would never rush into a decision until he became confident how God was leading. Surprisingly, he was a poor speaker and a hopeless linguist. Perhaps his early stutter had something to do with this. Lacking words, he would make them up: *teamu* for team, *highesti* for highest, *visioni, revivali*. Perhaps this weakness made him rely more on his African team, some of whom, notably William Nagenda and Festo Kivengere, were excellent linguists. Teamwork with his African brothers was integral to his evangelism, and they expanded his themes with vivid word-pictures. Whatever the reason, God graciously allowed his strength to be made perfect in Joe's weakness. When he spoke, people's hearts were stirred. What he said was simple and memorable. It came from his own heart and experience and it changed people's lives.

Another remarkable thing about Joe was the width of his vision. Already in the early days at Gahini, he would be looking far ahead and outwards in his prayers: 'Lord, you are blessing us here. We pray that your blessing of revival might spread outwards from this centre – to Uganda, to Kenya, to Tanganyika, to the world . . .' This might have seemed an exaggerated prayer. Now it was beginning to become reality. In March 1939, after a convention at Kinoni where the pastor was Erica Sabiti (later Archbishop of Uganda, Rwanda and Burundi), Joe revisited southern Sudan with Decie and William Nagenda. Revival had spontaneously broken out here, with many people being converted and village churches rapidly being built. As always, problems accompanied this fervour and, as Joe noted, 'We especially stressed the blood of Jesus in our messages as many had grown cold because of fruitless repenting . . .' A few missionaries were critical of what they saw as hysteria.

Joe's role here seemed to be to encourage the leaders and to bring biblical teaching into the situation.

Difficulties created by the revival were discussed among Ruanda Mission leaders at a special meeting at Ibuye in April when the fear was expressed of two groups or camps developing: the *Abaka* – 'those on fire' – and the rest. The theological basis of the revival was discussed, unity was re-affirmed, and the name *Abaka* began to be dropped. As Joe wrote to Mr Webster, General Secretary of the Mission, 'So far as I have been able to judge, *Abaka* as a name is no longer used, but the Revival, in its highest spiritual sense, will go forward purged of the errors and excesses which God has shown us are not of Him.'

The next move forward was an invitation for Joe and Lawrence Barham to take two teams to different parts of Tanganyika (Tanzania). Although it seemed at the time that there was little response, a week later Lionel Bakewell, the Australian CMS missionary who worked at Katoke, wrote that the people there had been transformed. In particular, he described Joe's use of a special gift which perhaps made up for his lack of eloquence:

Dr Church drew on the blackboard as he spoke. He drew on the left side of the board the Old Testament sacrifice for sin – a lamb on an altar of stones (blood drawn in red chalk), with a man kneeling in front of it. The way was repentance for sin and faith in the efficacy of the sacrifice. Then he drew on the right side a simple picture of our Lord on the Cross, the blood flowing down from his hands, feet and side, and a man kneeling at the foot of the Cross. The way was the same . . . without blood there is no cleansing from sin. This drawing and the accompanying message were the turning point of the mission. There was a deep hush, especially among the schoolboys as he drew the simple lines . . . That was the beginning of the most amazing transformation which has come to Katoke. God has

> literally visited his people . . . It has been to us a terrible revelation of the inner lives of those whom we had looked on as good Christians.

Once again, trouble followed the blessing. Strange things began to happen at Katoke. Two wives of missionaries at the Teacher Training School, following the teaching of a charismatically inclined Bible College in Wales where one of them had studied, began to teach that there must be *signs* following the outpouring of God's Spirit. Gradually things became completely out of hand, so that a year later, in April 1940, Bishop Chambers, who had invited Joe and the teams in the first place, wrote to Joe complaining, 'I am greatly disturbed over the confusion, disorder and unseemly conduct of meetings by the Africans, which Mr Bakewell regards as the work of the Holy Spirit and which he connects with your visit to Katoke.' Although Joe had already disassociated himself from these excesses, the Bishop ended, 'The revelation of the fruits of your mission force me to reconsider my invitation to you and your team to visit other parts of Tanganyika.' He failed to mention the positive fruits of revival – many released from the grip of drink, adultery, and the terrifying fear of witchcraft. Eventually, after much heartache and prayer, a balance was found: the outward signs were limited, but the work of God's Spirit went ahead. Charismatic gifts – speaking in tongues, and so on – were not normally as much in evidence in the revival as were changed lives.

Joe's work continued with a mission to Europeans in Kampala, ending with a service for large numbers in the cathedral. Britain declared war with Germany on Sunday 3 September and, back in Kabale, as Joe described, 'After the evening service we stood around the door of the big Kabale church in silence . . . Fearful thoughts went through our minds. Would the Italians invade Uganda from Ethiopia where they were thought to have big troop concentrations? We quickly gave our fears to the Lord and went about our duties but, as with news of a bereavement, everything from that moment changed.' Some missionaries joined up, but Joe wrote home, 'I am not anxious to join up as I did in the last war, as I believe God has given me a vision of a much more important war in which to engage here.' There were various changes at this time, including Joe's being put in charge of the Ruanda Mission's Bwama Island Leper Colony on Lake Bunyoni six miles from Kabale, and the dismantling of Kabale Hospital (there was now a good government hospital in Kabale) and its conversion to school buildings for Kigezi High School. Despite financial constraints, Joe got permission to retain and run one building as a small 'Pocket Hospital' for mission personnel and others who valued care in a Christian environment.

1940 brought with it both good things and bad. In August the first *Balokole* Convention was held at Namirembe, to give encouragement and clear Bible teaching to the increasing number of members of small scattered fellowships springing up within the churches all over Uganda and Ruanda. This highlighted a matter of constant concern to Joe and to many in the Ruanda Mission, the extent to which the Anglican church structure and clerical 'leadership on a pedestal', which was quite rigidly followed in the Church of Uganda, was appropriate in East Africa. Joe, a layman himself, and never hidebound by tradition, saw the immense value of the team ministry of laymen, black and white. As he put it, 'Everything depends on keeping the Fellowship really alive and burning within the visible church set-up, and then in time new life will change things irresistably.'

Closely linked with this concern was the spiritual quality of the clergy, and this brings us to events at Mukono Divinity School in October 1941, which became known as the

Mukono Crisis. The Bishop Tucker Memorial Theological College at Mukono, where Joe had been invited to lead a mission in 1936, was largely liberal in its approach, although some members of staff and several students were now *Balokole*. The situation there is well described by Bill Butler, 'captured' much to his own surprise by Joe a few years earlier to come out as one of the three who responded to the 'Uganda Seven' call, and now a very inexperienced tutor at the college:

> Many of the students in training had no assurance or even clear understanding of salvation. Most of them reflected the attitude widely prevailing in the Church of Uganda at that time, that provided they were baptized and confirmed and *not discovered* in any particular wrongdoing, they were Christians. Stealing in the college was rife as, to some extent, were drinking and immorality. Against this gloomy background a dozen or so students stood out sharply. Their faces shone. Their testimony, sometimes misunderstood, often resented, challenged all who heard it, as did their manner of life.

Among them were three ex-pupils of King's College, Budo: William Nagenda, Eleazar Mugimba and Erisa Wakabi, different indeed in spiritual, educational and leadership qualities from many of the other students. For them, as William wrote, 'Mukono is such a difficult place in every way. One can easily get cold . . .' As described already, since the death of Blasio Kigozi, William had been working with Joe at Gahini and travelling widely with him. Now at the age of 28 he had accepted an invitation from Bishop Stuart to train for the ministry at Mukono, as part of the Bishop's efforts both to encourage the revival and to recruit educated young men to the church's ministry. Through William and others, Bill Butler came into the experience of being 'broken' of wrong attitudes. He found forgiveness and a joyful coming into the light of full fellowship, and soon afterwards joined Joe, William, Simeon Nsibambi and others at a convention at Fort Portal in western Uganda. While there, Bill and the rest of the Mukono contingent became very convicted about the modernistic teaching and ritualistic innovations at the college and went back determined to check these things and to bring the college to repentance although, as Joe wrote, they had nothing personally against the Warden of the college, Mr Jones, whom they all liked. Bill continues the tale:

> Now the vision so clearly given had to be worked out in the day-to-day routine of a theological college. [Bishop Stuart] was very anxious lest the *Balokole* movement, with many of whose aims he was essentially in sympathy, might split the Church of Uganda . . . now I had to go and tell him that I believed God was leading me into total identification with it. Even more difficult was my interview with the Warden of Mukono, a brilliant scholar who had himself been blessed through the aftermath of the Welsh revival but had strangely little sympathy with what he regarded as a subversive movement.

After a spell in hospital with appendicitis, Bill came back to find himself transferred from the college. Two days later he heard that 26 students had been expelled as rebels and the African chaplain suspended. The immediate cause was the posting of three new regulations in the college, forbidding rising before 6 a.m., so that *Balokole* could no longer meet to pray at 4 a.m.; forbidding preaching within the college without permission from the Warden, and forbidding meetings of students in groups exceeding three. Recently the *Balokole* group had started preaching to their fellow students at 6 a.m. So their two most precious activities were being stopped. As Bill pointed out, these rules posed an agonizing choice to mature Christian students, many of them married men with families and within a few months of ordination:

> They pleaded with the College authorities to rescind the rules, but to no avail. They spent the half term holiday in prayer and fasting, before reaching the costly conclusion that in this particular situation they had no alternative but to obey God rather than man. The following morning they rose as usual for prayer and fellowship at 4 a.m. Their names were taken as they came from the meeting and submitted to the Warden. One by one they were solemnly expelled from the College, their licence to preach in the Church of Uganda withdrawn, and they were branded as rebels. The Bishop was away on safari at the time, or such severe measures might never have been taken.

One of the students expelled was William Nagenda. This serious event reflected on Joe's work and on the revival. The dismissed students and the chaplain were keen members of the group within the college who had been saved and helped during the June 1936 Mukono mission which Joe had led. Their vibrant and uncompromising faith was in large measure inspired by his teaching. As Bishop Stuart wrote to Joe shortly before the rift, 'It looks to me that we are approaching a crisis; for that crisis neither you nor I can be held completely innocent.' And to Joe it seemed that much as he condemned disobedience, 'The Warden seemed to have set a trap while the Bishop was out of the country, from which there was virtually no escape, for the twenty-six believed implicitly that they were being led by God to call the college to repentance before term ended.'

There was little the Bishop could do when he returned, but in December he wrote calling for prayer and for an emergency Diocesan Council to discuss 'the greatest crisis in the history of the Church of Uganda'. In December too, a group of *Balokole*, European and Ugandan, met at Kabale to discuss the situation. Their report concluded, 'We are unanimously convinced that the "Mukono incident" was unwisely handled and that the students were not in any true sense "rebels". They were technically guilty of disobedience to the warden's authority; but the issues at stake were far more important than any technicalities of college discipline and they were therefore justified in refusing to obey.'

Bishop Stuart was deeply hurt and blamed Joe and others for disloyalty in publishing and circulating this report without his knowledge. He expressed himself as saddened by the revival movement's criticisms of deadness in the Church of Uganda. While condemning the actions of the expelled students, he continued to welcome the revival, stating at the Synod of January 1942, 'It would be a sad day for the church if they were to be driven out and they never will be as long as I am Bishop, but I cannot prevent them from driving themselves out.' Mercifully this did not happen. But William and eight others saw in their expulsion from the college a clear call of God to step out in faith as free evangelists to Uganda while remaining within the church. William himself was offered a base for his evangelistic work at Namutamba, the tea plantation of one of the few white settlers in Uganda, Leslie Lea-Wilson, a friend of Joe's and a strong supporter of the Ruanda Mission. From this base William was to continue and develop a worldwide evangelistic ministry with Joe. Others went back to their professions as teachers or medical assistants and served as lay readers. All were highly mobile, travelling to hold evangelistic missions, visiting the brethren and building up the fellowships with which they were involved. As Joe commented, 'Why were some so slow to see that God might be wanting to do this very thing, and that it was not after all such a terrible tragedy?'

There were other troubles too. In July 1941 the Sudan Government had refused Joe a permit to enter the Sudan to conduct a mission with Bishop Gelsthorpe in Juba. He wrote to Bill Butler, 'I am amazed that the whole body of CMS from the Bishop downwards can allow this interference in purely spiritual things . . . Just because we allow Africans more equality and liberty on these teams it seems they are afraid. The result of treating the African as underdog is only too evident in S. Africa and Kenya, and surely the experiment of treating him as a brother Christian cannot be accompanied by any worse results than already exist!' He wrote too to Bishop Stuart, 'You and the Ruanda Mission have entrusted me with the running of conventions and missions for some years in Uganda, and now suddenly I find myself being suspect, spied upon (my letters are being censored) and barred from entering a neighbouring British Protectorate . . .' After a CMS Uganda Missionaries' Conference in Kampala in January 1942 which Joe sat in on as an observer, the criticism of the revival was such that Joe drove back to Kabale feeling as though he had been beaten and wondering what plans there were to get him out of Kabale. Bewildered, he wrote in his diary, 'They had prayed for revival and now it has come they turn round and fight it. Revival leaders have been moved to outlandish spots. I have a feeling sometimes that God has some plan to set me free so that I can visit and help the bands of *Balokole* all over Uganda.'

Despite the difficulties, 1942 was perhaps the peak of the revival, as Joe drove his 'teamus' around Kigezi. It was at this time that Festo Kivengere came as a teacher to Kigezi High School and joined the teams. Driving around with Joe, their fellowship became very close. Festo was amazed at the way Joe was prepared to discuss personal problems and failures with his African team members, who in their turn were prepared to open up. At first, Joe would preach in

English and Festo would interpret for him into various local languages, all of which he spoke fluently. Joe soon discovered that Festo was 'very bright at getting to know my way of saying things', and soon they were co-operating more and more, with Festo often adding comment or personal testimony. Their personalities fitted together well. Both were ardent evangelists and Joe loved Festo's bubbly enthusiasm. They became like brothers. It was a great loss to the *teamus* and to Joe personally when in 1945 Festo was called to work in Tanganyika.

In October 1942, as a result of a misunderstanding between Joe and the Bishop over the possibility of Joe's instituting a yearly convention in Uganda for the deepening of spiritual life, the Bishop suspended Joe from preaching anywhere in Uganda except Kigezi and officially removed his lay reader's licence. It seemed that things could hardly get much worse. Joe wrote in his private diary, 'These are some of the most difficult days of my life, but yet God gives me absolute peace. I found Kenya full of friends in the Lord from all missions but the Keswick committee were afraid of me and banned me. Then at Kabale I have slowly had to hand over everything to Len and Esther [Sharp].' He even feared that his beloved 'European school' would be rebuilt, using Eileen's gift, at Ibuye instead of at Kabale, but this did not happen.

The trouble with the Bishop began with a warning letter dated 22 May 1942 in which, still addressing him as Joe, he wrote, 'I feel [revival] is being held up and will be held up until you and the people who left Mukono make a complete and public apology for the Kabale report and their actions at Mukono and since . . . Joe can't you see the tragedy of this thing you and your friends have done? God enables you to start a work and then you go and destroy it – and all as far as I can see from sinful pride.' Then on 2 October came an official letter as follows:

Dear Dr Church,
I am informed that for the second time in six weeks you have tried to go behind my back and except for the refusal of members of this mission to back up your dishonesty, you would have arranged a convention here and booked the Kiwala hotel for that purpose. If my information is correct, I have no alternative but to withdraw your licence to preach in this mission or hold any meetings until you repent of your dishonesty. I have the honour to be your obedient servant, etc.

Joe replied, explaining that he had only been *enquiring* about the possibility of booking the Kiwala on behalf of a group of missionaries from Kenya, Uganda and Ruanda who had expressed interest in holding a 'Keswick' convention. In fact nothing had been booked, as it was found to be much too expensive. If it had been, Joe fully intended to speak to the Bishop about it first. It seemed that three Namirembe missionaries had heard Joe talking about this and had reported back, mistakenly, that Joe had intended to go behind the Bishop's back. The Bishop was not convinced. Algie Stanley Smith then entered the fray, writing to the Bishop pointing out that his qualification 'If my information is correct' did suggest that he felt an element of doubt, and assuring the Bishop of Joe's good faith. He asked the Bishop to withdraw his letter of 2 October, pointing out that it was the devil's plan to keep the Bishop and Joe in opposition: 'For God's sake, don't let him play his game.'

Algie also wrote to Joe, pointing out some justification for the Bishop's annoyance with Joe in that Joe seemed not to realize that arranging a convention in Uganda was different from doing it in Kenya because in Uganda there was only one national church with the Bishop at its head. He went on, 'For the moment you must accept his ban on your activities in Uganda outside Kigezi. Our policy must be to realize that the living church has two sections, one the organized institutional body, and the other the living witnessing inner circle. Both are necessary, and trouble has been caused in the past by the inner circle despising the big institution and considering it more or less unnecessary.'

In a further letter to the Bishop, Joe reiterated that he had had no intention of booking the Kiwala without consulting him. He added that he agreed to the Bishop's veto and the removing of his licence, that he was sorry for anything he had done wrong and for his 'tactless and blundering methods', and that he had never intended to start a battle, having always been anxious to avoid any split between the *Balokole* and the Uganda church. He wrote too about a gathering at Kamwezi, when careful teaching had been given to try to curb some of the excesses of the revival, like the noisy repenting during services.

As the Bishop began to seek a 'New Way' forward, the question of whether a formal apology should be made for the Kabale report caused much heart-searching. Many letters went back and forth. In February 1943 Algie Stanley Smith wrote to Joe about the need to acknowledge humbly and frankly faults in the past, adding, 'I believe it will be your hardest battle, Joe old man. I do pray you won't shirk it. You must be broken on this. If you will see it yourself and get William [Nagenda] to see it, you will have done a great thing.' At about the same time, Erica Sabiti wrote to Joe saying that he was willing to repent of anything which was wrong in the Report but that he didn't see anything to repent of. Leslie Lea-Wilson too felt the Report should stand, although publishing it without the Bishop's knowledge had been discourteous.

At a gathering at Ibuye at the end of February, Joe and others couldn't help feeling that the Bishop's attempts to reach unity were based on human effort and were an attempt to control the revival. At the same time, praying earnestly for help, they too experienced what they felt was God's 'new way'. As Joe wrote later to the Bishop, 'For me personally those days were terribly humbling. I saw that I had let down the cause of revival and the life of victory that I had preached about, by carelessness and lack of victory in my own life. Practically this new way for me is to endeavour to cease all self-vindicating and "waiting for the other man to repent first" attitude and to go forward myself aiming for Christ's highest standards.' Sorrow and regret was expressed to the Bishop by the four Ruanda Mission signatories of the Kabale Report that the report had caused such great trouble, especially having been printed without his knowledge. To the Bishop it seemed that all barriers between himself and the revival group were broken down and he personally restored Joe's licence. The 'New Way' initiative did not find general acceptance with the *Balokole*, William Nagenda in particular affirming strongly that unity with the liberal Church of Uganda approach was not 'the Highest'. Nonetheless it was remarkable that these events did not result in a major schism between the revival movement and the church. By the 1950s, as Joe had always hoped and believed to be possible, the revival had become an integral part of the life of the church of Uganda. (Letters quoted here all in File *Licence Removed 1942 and The New Way 1943*, Joe Church archive.)

In May 1943, despite Decie's having been involved in a nasty accident in January when the car which she was driving with Robin in it turned upside down on the steep road down to Lake Bunyoni, Joe and Decie's fifth child was born – the longed-for daughter, Janine. A need had arisen once again for a doctor at Gahini so, soon after Janine's birth, Joe embarked on a new and difficult pattern of life, working one month in every three at Gahini, and travelling between two homes. On 19 May he wrote, 'Here I am alone – once again on the ant-ridden, malarial hill of Gahini. Everything is in an awful state, except the spiritual work. How good God has been to us since Decie and I were married 13 years ago today.' And in June, again at Gahini, 'Yesterday was a landmark in my life. For years I have longed for the day when I would see revival bring fruit within the Church of England. Yesterday we had a reformed C of E communion service. It was a deep and unforgettable time of blessing.'

In 1944, after a painful meeting of the Uganda Church Synod in Kampala where the Bishop described the revival in terms of 'rebels' and 'disobedience' in the presence of the Kabaka (King of Buganda – a part of Uganda) and the Governor of Uganda, Joe travelled to South Africa with Lawrence Barham and Dr Godfrey Hindley – permits for black leaders had been refused – to take the revival message there. They spoke in a packed church in Cape Town, but there only Europeans were present. They went on to meet the 'coloureds' in their church and the Africans in theirs, but made it plain that they could not envisage revival in South Africa if the African brothers were kept separate. While he was in South Africa, a message reached Joe to say that his mother, whose love and encouragement had meant so much to him, had died in wartime England.

In July 1945 a three-day gathering was held at Byumba in the mountains of northern Ruanda. Small groups sat on and on, totally absorbed in testimony, prayer and quiet singing. Joe came across 'one group where some Banyaruanda and Bachiga were dancing for joy. Then one said, "For years we have only crossed that valley into Uganda with spears for fear of being killed. Now God has made us one . . . *Tukutendereza Yesu*!"'. He described too how

Sunday was a remarkable day on this hilltop in a forest of eucalyptus trees as the crowd listened to Psalm 22. When we had finished the crowd would not disperse, and one by one people asked to speak. One was a dignified Mututsi sub-chief named

Kilimenti Semugabo, a nominal Roman Catholic, whose eyes God had opened, who shared with us a dream. This was the dream of the bowed head of Christ, bowed in submission three times as he accepted his father's will to come to earth, to be rejected and crucified, and to suffer separation from his Father as he bore the weight of the sin of the world. Each time, Kilimenti bowed his head as he said the words, 'Yes, Father'. Then he said, 'I saw Christ dying for me, I found myself gazing at him on the Cross as he bowed his head for my sins, and I heard a voice saying to me, "Are you a thief?" But quickly I stiffened my neck and said, "No, I'm not. It's only what everyone does!" Then as I looked at the One on the Cross looking down at me my heart melted, and I bowed my head to him and said, "Yes, Lord, I am a thief. It is I who should have died, not you." '

As Joe commented, 'This dream that must have come from the Spirit of God has gone round the world, and has become one of the basic messages of the East African Revival.' It was also the basis of the 'Bowed neck' motto cards, first devised with Joe's invaluable pin-men, which encapsulated revival teaching.

In September 1945 the second Kabale convention took place (the first, in 1935, had been the starting point of revival in Uganda), and in February 1946 the Ruanda Mission celebrated its silver jubilee. Algie Stanley Smith referred to the Kabale convention the previous September, when 'On the Kabale hill where we found that tiny handful of believers, a convention gathered last September of some fifteen thousand people, not the product of a mass movement, but drawn by the heart-hunger of a church throbbing with spiritual life.' As so often seemed to be the case, even these large conventions became a source of criticism, as the Bishop of Uganda became concerned that formal Christmas and Easter celebrations of Holy Communion were being omitted as huge numbers of Christians attended the conventions. He felt duty-bound to report Joe personally to the Archbishop of Canterbury, as being responsible for seriously undermining the structure of the Anglican Church in Uganda. The Archbishop read the booklet *Jesus Satisfies* – the story of the Kabale conventions – which Joe promptly sent him, and wisely replied to the Bishop confirming the need for church discipline but acknowledging, 'It is clear that there is a real revival and a notable work of evangelism going on in Ruanda', so Joe was vindicated.

At long last on 19 June 1946, Joe and Decie and their five children set off on a troopship for leave in post-war England. For the two eldest, John and David, childhood and family life in Africa had come to an end.

15

1946–1958: Post-War Change and Growth

By 1946 much had changed. For Joe and Decie's children their Kabale idyll had already begun to shatter. One by one the boys had had to leave Kabale Preparatory School and the security of home when they reached the age of 10 and travelled a 3–4 day journey by car and train to 'proper school' – for John and David it was Nairobi Primary School, a preparatory school for settlers' children in Kenya. John had been the first to make this journey in 1941, and David joined him in 1942. Joe and Decie would drive them the 300 miles to Kampala, combining the journey with essential shopping, visits to the dentist, and so on. One night would be spent with Roy and Dora Billington – Dr Roy Billington was a doctor at Mengo Hospital – and then the boys were put on the big steam train, which took two days and a night to reach Nairobi. It was an exciting journey, the boys running down the station in the middle of the night while the stokers were at work and jumping up in the cab with the engine driver, running back again at the next station. In Nairobi they stayed with an architect's family, the Archers, who took in day-boys as lodgers, sleeping them in small *bandas* [cabins] in their garden, four or five 'banda boys' in each. For David it was a traumatic time: bullying and homosexual practices were rife; his parents were hundreds of miles away and it was almost impossible to convey to them what was going on. Somehow he survived – he had inherited a quality of courage and determination from his father. Two years later, at twelve, the boys moved on to the Prince of Wales School, also in Nairobi – very colonial, with most of the pupils children of farmers and pioneers.

In 1946, with the war over, it was possible at last to go to England. The family travelled home in a troopship, the *Winchester Castle* – 700 people on board, with men and boys in bunks three deep, one above the other, and women and girls 16 to a cabin. In England much had changed. Despite the widespread relief, it was a time of austerity, exhaustion and loss. Joe's parents, Florence and Edward, had both died, although both had survived almost to the end of the war with remarkable cheerfulness and courage. In 1938 they had regretfully left Fen Ditton and retired to Ridlands Cottage, Limpsfield. During the eight years that they were at Fen Ditton they had provided a remarkable, welcoming base for the family. Over that period Christine (Wizz) and Betty were still unmarried and at home, together with Violet and her husband Kenneth who was working in Cambridge. All four rallied round to help Edward and Florence run the large rectory and parish. The rest of the family were serving God in various parts of the world, finding their life-partners, marrying, producing babies – Florence and Edward had 30 grandchildren eventually – and coming back to Fen Ditton periodically where the 'home team' loved and nurtured them. Edward and Florence revelled in sharing this lovely place with the family, and could hardly believe that God had given it to them, with its beautiful garden and the favoured terrace from which was seen the best Ditton Corner view of the boat races. Not surprisingly, they were popular too with CICCU and other members of the university.

It was during the Fen Ditton years that the Church family letter was circulated, and it draws a happy picture of Florence and Edward as the loving and prayerful hub of a whirl of activity. As Edward wrote in it in 1935, 'We have our moments of pride as well as of thankfulness in the old home when we read of all your doings in distant lands. Compared with your busy lives, our own seems very quiet and unimportant in this country parish, but we have our hands very full.' They were appreciated by their children, and Joe wrote from Gahini that same year, 'I think we all ought to feel very proud of Pater and Mater . . . What would we all do without Fen Ditton?'

From the secure centre of Fen Ditton the family letter, housed in four strongly bound exercise books, circulated the world. It reached and was added to by Mary and Rupert Penn at St John's College, Palamcottah, South India; Daisy and Dick Schor in Montevideo, Uruguay, where Dick was not only headmaster of the British Boys' School, but also Correspondent to *The Times*, covering the Bolivian/ Paraguayan Chaco War; Howard as he worked with the CMS at Kabare in Kenya and married Lizzo Reichwald who had helped his sisters with girls' Broads cruises; Bill as he followed Joe to Ruanda and then moved on to Urundi, marrying a fellow missionary Janet Casson; George who was ordained and went on to be a well-known RAF padre and chaplain to the Queen, marrying Helen Langhard of Switzerland; and Joe and Decie themselves. Scattered as they were, the letter drew them together with news, photographs and requests for prayer.

The letter ceased to circulate with the outbreak of war; it was feared that it would be torpedoed on its travels. And Edward and Florence moved to Ridlands Cottage with Christine and Betty. They emphasized that the various families would be as welcome as ever in the much smaller house, as long as they didn't all come at once! It wasn't a peaceful spot to be, as German bombers constantly droned overhead on their way from the south coast to London. Often they would jettison their bombs on the hills around Limpsfield. But when Wizz eventually moved away, and Betty was out all day teaching in a nearby school, Florence and Edward went quietly on, reading to each other in the shelter when there were 'strangers' about, going out to pick mushrooms and anything else they could find to supplement their limited diet. They firmly put their trust in God and refused to be evacuated to a safer place.

But now, within five months of each other they had gone to be with the heavenly Father whom they had trusted and loved. And with the war over, the families who had been abroad were coming back (all at once) and needing somewhere to stay. The Penns were back already – they had left India for the sake of their children's schooling in 1935 and were living Beech Cottage nearby. Ridlands Cottage had been established under a Trust, the idea being for the expatriate members of the family to have somewhere to stay with their children. But now it was bursting at the seams, with the Schors, as well as Bill and his family in residence. For Joe and Decie's five children, fun though it was to meet the cousins, it was not easy to adjust. As David, who was sleeping in the garage, remembers, 'England came as a shock to us. Everything was so much smaller, the clouds so much closer, suddenly the whole world was tiny, and so cramped.' Michael too, only eight at the time, found England very constricting, with its hedges and barbed wire. 'And why do they say, "Trespassers will be persecuted"?', he wondered. He, like Robin, hated St Michael's School where he was sent nearby, and ran away. The snow of the cold winter of 1947 was exciting; the mumps which they all caught was not such fun. Decie, used to Africa, found it hard to shop and cook for so many single-handed. Altogether it was a difficult time. In 1947 Joe's sister Betty also came home on leave after the war. In August 1941 she had married Dr Bill Young, a dashing Rugby Blue at St Catharine's College, Cambridge, and a Scottish International player; they were working with the Africa Inland Mission in Kenya.

Joe, as always, used every moment of his time in Europe. In January 1947 he, Lawrence Barham and Bill Butler responded to an invitation from Berthe Ryf, a missionary nurse who had found revival blessing in Ruanda, to take the same message to her home country, Switzerland. In England too, Joe led revival teams of witness in several parishes, culminating with William Nagenda and Yosiya Kinuka joining the team and speaking at the Keswick Convention. The official Keswick report commented, 'It was heart-stirring to see the shining face of William Nagenda, an African Christian from Uganda, and to hear him tell of the Revival there.'

At the end of 1947 Joe, Decie and their three younger children returned to Ruanda. This time they went to Gahini (nearly 20 years since Joe first went there), to live in the old mission house, to continue the medical work, to help Yosiya pastoring the 300 village churches in the area, and to begin to rebuild the whole hospital in more permanent materials. John, aged sixteen and David, fifteen, were left in England to continue their education at St Lawrence College, Ramsgate, Joe's old school. The trauma of being left to cope in what was virtually a foreign country, cold and grey, was an extra burden of anxiety. While in England, Decie had been diagnosed as having breast cancer and was operated on. David remembers his parents visiting them during their first term at St Lawrence, and walking along the beach with himself and John, telling them about Decie's illness. Then they went, shortly to leave for Africa. The boys said goodbye, unsure whether they would ever see their mother again. Joe and Decie trusted God unswervingly and prayed for healing. Their faith was vindicated; the tumour proved benign. Decie made a complete recovery, thereafter to be fitted with a somewhat roving prosthesis much to the amusement of the family.

The first thing to be done on their arrival was to pack up the family home at Kabale and move everything to Gahini. Janine, then four and a half, remembers the journey:

> Everything was piled into an enormous open lorry, with Aunt Flo's tin bath on top. The bath fell off after the customs checking and repacking at the border, and was dented forever. It was one of the many wedding presents which Decie had carefully collected together during the two-year engagement, before sailing for Africa to join Joe. As well as household goods we were transporting our animals. The muscovy ducks travelled in the trailer behind our car, with the family boat inverted over them. At one point in the journey a wheel of the trailer came off, and it was Michael, who always seemed to have just what was needed in his pockets, who saved the day by producing a nail which fixed the wheel back. Dawn had broken when we arrived at Gahini.

For John and David left in England, a time of extraordinary difficulty now began, and a pattern was set which was to be followed by all four boys over the next 15 years or so. They were virtually left to fend for themselves, with John having a chequebook, paying the bills and being responsible for his younger brother. They made their own holiday arrangements, choosing which of the relations – some they found more congenial than others – to stay with, and joining the Walrus cruises which Joe had started long before. Effectively John left home at sixteen, and saw himself through school and university, visiting his parents at Gahini only once for a Cambridge long vacation, because money was short. A loyal and responsible eldest child, he suffered desperate loneliness and insecurity without complaint. His letters home were full of the usual schoolboy banalities as he didn't want to worry his parents. There was no one with whom he could share his feelings. Amazingly he remained loyal, accepting that his father needed to be faithful to his vision of 'the Highest' no matter what turmoil it caused his ever-loyal wife and family. David, younger and with less responsibility, suffered less, forming a strong attachment to his Aunt Marjorie in Devon once Granny Tracey died, and regarding Willand where he was born as his English home. Hard though it was, there was lots of fun too, as the large family clan and other Christian groups of young people got together for sailing on the Broads, picnics, campfires and so on. The Church boys, enjoying games, brought up with swimming and boats, playing their guitars, were always popular.

Back at Gahini, Joe and his team travelled more and more, responding to invitations to take the gospel and the revival message back to Switzerland, to Germany, to France, to Nyasaland (Malawi), to Angola and to India. Decie meanwhile looked after Janine and the two younger boys when they were at home and held the fort at Gahini. With Joe so often away, Decie's help was often needed at the hospital. She also did the accounts for the whole mission station, spending hours counting out Belgian francs, the Ruanda currency for wages; and she ran women's groups as well. Two other things took up much of her time. One was gardening, which she loved and at which she became very expert. Fruit trees, vegetables and flowers all flourished under her green fingers. Then there were the letters which Decie lovingly and faithfully wrote weekly to her children now that they were separated. Sometimes, particularly once all four boys were in England, she would write one letter giving her and Joe's news and send copies to each, but always the last page would be left blank and there she would comment encouragingly on each boy's particular news. Each letter would end warmly 'with lots of love from your own Mum'. The children found it difficult to share their real feelings with their parents in response, although later on Joe wrote to Michael thanking him for letting them come in on his 'ups and downs, and little bits of inner news'. Joe added, 'I feel I let down *my* parents in this way. I used to like to spring little surprises on them which, as I look back, was just selfishness and unbrokenness. Mum and I will try to let you into our inner feelings, especially as we get older. Old people are often closed books!' Looking back many years later, Michael felt that Decie's letters had been wonderfully factual, giving all their latest news, but that they never got very deep or related to his own immediate problems. All in all, he felt he never established a real relationship with his mother, partly because Decie rarely did show her feelings, aware though she was that 'natural reserve can be a great hindrance'. Isolated from much that she loved – art and music – for Joe's sake and for their life's work, she remained quietly cheerful, her silent motto, 'I have learned, in whatever state I am, to be content' (Phil. 4:11).

For Janine, the move from Kabale to Gahini brought the pain of separation too, for Kabale Preparatory School, which had been a blissful 'school at home' for the boys, was now 75 miles away. From the age of five and a half she was sent there as a boarder. At first, Michael was there as well, but for 3 months at a time she did not see her parents, even at half-term. Eileen Faber, Michael and Janine's godmother, did her best to mother her, but she left soon. She married Hercules Pakenham, a provincial commissioner, who had been severed from his missionary parents at the age of two, and saw his father only twice in 18 years. All the 'aunties' were very kind. At half-terms and holidays they arranged fabulous outings – whole-day picnics on Sharp's Island reached by canoe, lovely walks with picnic lunch and tea. It was a happy school, but even so the little girl was beset by fears, of which she spoke to no one. Her letters home were very short – a line or two and a picture. They gave no hint of her anxieties. And yet at night she was often petrified, hearing noises and seeing moving lights (simply the housegirls going back to their quarters, she later realized) which she could not understand. One night, in terror she prayed for help. Then, as she lay rigid with eyes wide open, she saw something – someone coming down to her in a basket, and she knew it was Jesus and was calmed and reassured.

Robin and then Michael left KPS and moved on to Kenton College in Nairobi, remembering

> the great train climbing, climbing slowly and then gadunk-a-dunk down the escarpment, fruit-sellers on the stations, bunk beds (exciting top ones), posh meals in the restaurant car, magic views of the Rift Valley, dear Aunt Vera – fleeting visit and small present, Aunt Lizzo – big heart- and Uncle Howard – quiet and distant – in their Nairobi home. The school wasn't all bad – wonderful grounds, marbles, roller skates, dens, half-term visits to the Game Park and the Ngong Hills, Aunt Lizzo nearby – a great encourager – and at last the rising excitement of the long journey home and arriving at Gahini in the dark – wonderful.

Joe taught them all to be *gufu* (Swahili for 'strength') children with a stiff upper lip, so they never complained but made the best of things. Robin reckoned that their difficulties encouraged independence, and he concentrated on the good times, of which there were many. He would come off the train laden with guinea pigs and other special things which he had bought on the journey. So the years rolled by. Janine gives a picture of daily life at Gahini:

> We had a large staff – housegirls, cook, their helpers, carpenters. There was someone to look after the poultry and rabbits

which we relied on for meat, a gardener for near the house and another for the irrigated vegetables and banana plantation down by the lake. We needed them all to maintain our self-sufficient lifestyle, but we were also providing a living for several families, as well as the careful training in hygiene and household management which my mother gave the housegirls. A few things like tea, sugar, salt and soap were bought every three months and stored in dustbins. In the dry season, water was brought up from the lake on porters' heads and collected in the tank. Some meat we bought from the market at the top of the hill – beef or a whole live sheep which was skinned, divided and shared. Fish was brought by fishermen from the lake. Milk was brought in a churn every day from the cows on the hill. Often greatly diluted, it had to be tested with a hydrometer. It smelt of the cows' urine in which the gourds which held it were washed, and it had to be boiled, but the resulting cream was good. Eventually we got our own cow.

After an early cup of tea and 'quiet times' there was breakfast on the veranda – porridge and cream, egg and toast [The quiet time was the essential start of Joe and Decie's day, when drawing close to God by reading the Bible and prayer, they found strength and guidance for whatever the day might bring. Decie stayed in bed for hers, Joe went down to his study.] Then after short family prayers, Joe dashed off up the hill to the hospital on his bike, to reappear for a cooked lunch and again for tea. Once a week we had prayers for all the staff in the living room. We children were looked after by the *ayah* [maid] between breakfast and lunch, while Decie concentrated on mission and household affairs. We loved the *ayahs*, they always had time for us. Mum and I were very much on the same wavelength and I loved doing things with her. Each home leave she bought enough Liberty lawn fabric to make dresses for herself and for me for the next four years. So in the holidays out came the old Singer sewing machine. I turned the handle and she'd guide the fabric. It was great fun. Another good time was siesta. I'd lie beside Mum on their big double bed and she would read to me. All the best children's books were sent out to us once a year by Aunt Lil.

Janine had few playmates. Apart from a few handpicked families like Yosiya Kinuka's, play with the African children was not particularly encouraged and the language barrier made it difficult. At the times when Bill was working with Joe at Gahini, there were all the cousins to play with, and that was wonderful. When Michael was there, that was wonderful too, and sometimes they would be allowed down to the lake and would spend hours out on the water in the boat. Target shooting and collecting eggs and butterflies were other things they loved. But if a car coming round the lake warned of visitors, Janine would be off like a frightened deer, hiding in the chicken houses or with the rabbits until all was clear. Once or twice in a week might come a family picnic by the lake – pure joy. Other special times were the evenings when after tea Joe, Decie and the children would walk together in the evening cool, inspecting the day's building work and enjoying the beauty and peace. Other evening rituals were Joe's going round the house swatting the malaria-transmitting mosquitoes, the baths which they all took in the famous tin bath, now set in concrete and fitted with taps through which came water from the tank heated outside on wooden fires, and the careful covering up of legs and arms for the evening against mosquito attack, with the long housecoats which Decie made. Janine has given a picture of her mother:

She was calm and even tempered, with a lovely peaceful smile. She was not a great talker, unlike the rest of the Tracey family who would talk non-stop all at once. She was an excellent organizer. Just occasionally if life got on top of her she would become tearful and retreat to her bedroom, but this was rare.

One such occasion was when my father had some bushes cut down because they were overgrown and obstructing the view of the lake, without consulting her first. All the plants were precious to her, and she was devastated. Her appearance never changed – hair up and parted in the middle, Liberty lawn dresses and open Clark's sandals. She found the revival difficult to cope with, and often used me as an excuse to get out of long meetings. For example on Christmas morning, she and I only stayed for the first hour of the three-hour service. Then, feeling wonderfully naughty, we would escape into the bright sunshine. She was happier doing quietly practical things – making up carefully chosen parcels of clothes sent out from England for all the Gahini families at Christmas time, leading a women's sewing group on the lawn with prayers and a Bible reading.

Janine too found the revival threatening. There was the oppressive fear of what would happen if you did not do the things you were expected to do, like reading your Bible every day. And then the constant fear of being challenged about your spiritual state. Being shy, she could not always answer satisfactorily, and so the whole thing made her nervous. Joe, though immensely proud of his daughter, was disappointed. He would have loved her to testify at the revival meetings. Meanwhile, Joe himself was working much too hard, 'like a puppy chasing its own tail'. As he realized, 'It's quite easy to let Gahini kill you!' To his African friends he was in danger of *gufuba* – striving too much – needing peace.

By 1951 John was studying medicine and David, reluctant to follow the family pattern of medicine at Emmanuel and Bart's, went back to Gahini for two years while making up his mind what to do. The Belgian Government in Ruanda had earmarked some money for rebuilding Gahini Hospital, and David, who already shared Joe's love of building, concentrated on this, setting Joe free to travel and to preach. It was a great help, and a wonderful time for David, back in Africa which to him was home. Janine, now aged eight, found it hard to relate to this grown-up brother whom she hardly knew. Snippets from Decie's diary give a picture of their lives at this time:

12 Jan. Helped Joe with a Caesarean. Visiting patients. Picnic tea by the lake, bathing from boat.

21 Feb. A Mututsi woman, a widow whose husband had died of TB, after hearing the pathology report that her son also had TB, went down to the lake and drowned herself. Joe and David rushed out with a boat but couldn't find her.

24 Feb. Body of woman found floating where they draw water.

4 March. Walk with David. Sang and played harmonium in the evening.

7 March. Typing list of workmen's names. Took all morning, when not interrupted.

13 March. Attempts to write letters all day, with many interruptions.

31 March. Michael arrived here from school 7.45 p.m.

4 April. Joe to Kabale to fetch Janine.

14 May. Expedition to Warthog Ridge, due east from Gahini. Saw a herd of zebra in the valley. On the way back shot two partridges.

18 May. Thieves had been in the night and made a hole in the side wall of the bookshop with a hammer and chisel taken from the carpenters' shop cupboard. Many things were taken, chiefly rice, and Joe's bike off the front veranda. Joe and David went off in the car and tracked the bike wheel marks and the spilt rice for over 20 miles, where they overtook the thief with the bike. David gave chase and caught him after about half a mile. They took him to Kibungu prison (he had escaped earlier while serving a sentence).

The news of dramatic events like the drowning of the woman in the lake and the stealing of the rice were brought by Priscilla, a woman with shrivelled legs who had been converted at the hospital and was given a job sweeping the verandas. Early every morning she would be sweeping and singing praises to God, but on 21 February Joe, up early to pray, heard her singing to herself, 'It might have been me . . . praise the Lord it wasn't me . . . went down to the lake and just walked on into the sea . . .' and similarly on 18 May he woke to the alarming refrain, 'Don't you know, they've stolen all the rice.' The beaming Priscilla was an excellent bearer of the daily news. She illustrates too the determination of Joe and all at Gahini to try to establish people in useful work. Every Monday morning there would be a line-up, when ex-patients would come looking for work and if possible they would be given a suitable job, like the amputees who sat on grass mats weeding the flower beds and gravel paths, or the people with elephantiasis who dug out ant-heaps as they had no feeling in their legs and feet. One man, Zabandora the gardener, was eventually in his old age employed solely to clean Joe's car.

John's visit for the summer of 1951 included a wonderful week when the family lived in tents down by the lake. Then in 1952 came a worrying time when David, who had become something of a local hero after catching the thief, was seriously ill with a high temperature and pains in his chest. As David drifted in and out of delirium, Joe was faced with a dilemma, as he was booked to visit India for the first time with William Nagenda. The call had seemed very clear, so Joe set off as planned in faith, trusting God that David would pull through. After what Decie described as 'a hectic day: packing for Michael, nursing David, packing for Joe, preparing picnic for journey', Joe set off, launching Michael back to school on the way.

India seemed ready for the revival message. Some

missionaries who had heard what God was doing in East Africa had already been touched by it, and the EFI (Evangelical Fellowship of India) had been launched with the aim of uniting the various Christian groups through spiritual revival. It was the EFI who invited Joe and William to India, the chairman writing, 'The need of India is desperate, the churches from one end of the land to the other are full of nominalism, strife, immorality and sin'. And the secretary of EFI also wrote to Joe, referring to the remarkable blessing already experienced and adding, 'all of us feel that the flame has leapt the seas'. As Joe described, 'Sitting in the plane William and I lay back in our seats as darkness settled over the Arabian desert. We prayed together, "O Lord Jesus, forgive us for coldness and lack of burden for the lost. Give us a deep love of India and may many step out on to the highway of holiness with thee, and walk with thee for ever." And so we slept, suspended above the stars.'

They landed in Madras, determined not to speak about the Ruanda revival, but simply to preach 'Jesus Christ and him crucified'. They were stunned by the heat and the terrible poverty they saw. Almost at once William was driven to protest and got out of a rickshaw saying he could not allow himself to be pulled by a sweating dark-skinned brother. As they travelled from place to place throughout the vast country their prayers were answered. 'Everywhere we found the same melting power of the cross as in East Africa, as we spoke often in weakness, an African and an Englishman, sharing rooms and travelling together, fellow wayfarers along the highway of the victorious life.'

After much blessing, they returned to Gahini. David was not only fully recovered, but had made great progress with the rebuilding. It was work he loved, grass-roots architecture. He and the team of African builders made bricks down by the lake and fired them; they dug natural paint pigments from the hillsides and boiled them up in 40-gallon drums.

Mortar was made from local mud and ant-heaps. The buildings were planned with loving care to fit in with the surroundings. David got to know the Africans well. He knew that when they started teasing him, 'We know why you work so much harder than we do – you eat meat', it was time to stop work for a day and go hunting instead. A water-buck would be shot and then all would share in a huge barbecue, with not a scrap wasted. By the time Joe returned from India, David had completed the new headmaster's house for the school. As well as building work, David had his own studio and built up a small trade in painting local views. Sometimes he would sit quietly and paint on the lake in the canoe he had built, the birds and animals intrigued to see a human being so still. Gradually his way forward became clear and he went on to study architecture in Oxford and then to spend ten years in Kenya and Uganda, designing schools, hospitals, churches and cathedrals and other key buildings, including the Bank of Uganda, in the vital post-independence years.

In June a big 'Jubilee convention' was held at Gahini. In 1952 too, news of the Mau Mau troubles in Kenya had burst upon the world. Joe was not involved directly, although his brother Howard, a missionary in Kenya, was. But the East African Revival had immeasurably strengthened many Christians in Kenya, many of whom stood up to the Mau Mau gangs with great bravery, refusing to take the Mau Mau oath, so that Cecil Bewes, later Africa Secretary for the CMS, was able to write,

We praise God for this revival, without which there would be very little left of the Kikuyu church. It has brought new life to thousands. It is a return to the simple gospel of the cross of Jesus. This is the most thrilling fellowship that I ever met in my life, a fellowship that surpasses all barriers of colour and race. Africans have confessed that they used to hate Europeans until they came to know them as brothers in Christ. It is not for nothing that the Kikuyu church was recalled – just in time – to a new emphasis on the precious blood of Jesus.

The writer Jeremy Murray-Brown too observed, in his biography of Jomo Kenyatta, that 'The full brunt of Mau Mau terrorism fell on the Kikuyu themselves – and especially upon Christians. Most of these African Christians were deeply affected by the East African Revival which swept into Kenya from Ruanda in 1949. They now stood up to the threats, tortures and cruelties of the Mau Mau gangs with a bravery which humbled and inspired their European missionaries' (*Kenyatta*, London: George Allen & Unwin, 1972, p. 282).

In July 1952, Joe and William flew to Europe for their third tour. In August Decie, David, Michael and Janine sailed back to England – a wonderful trip via the Cape – for a two-year stay in England, as Joe and William together with Roy Hession and his wife Revel were invited for a preaching tour to America and Canada in 1953. In the same year Joe and William also visited France, Switzerland and Israel and in 1954 he and William revisited India. For Janine this home leave meant two years at St Michael's School – one of them a difficult year as a boarder, the other cycling as a day-girl from Ridlands Cottage. For Michael it was an even harder wrenching from all that was home, as he started at St Lawrence College, Ramsgate. He was twelve, and although Joe and Decie stayed in England several times, he was to revisit Gahini only once during his teenage years. As he wrote many years later, separation was his most persistent experience. Although he found kindness, happiness and fun in England, it left him with a carapace of sadness as he grieved for so much left behind – his parents, his sister, his East African childhood. Once back at Gahini, Decie wrote to him faithfully, and these letters continue the story of her and Joe's lives. '1 February 1955. Dad has been doing some jobs on the boats. They have not been kept up to the standard that he would like, as you can guess, so there's plenty to be done. It is very lovely down there now . . . Are you fixed up for the Broads cruise in April? John said he hoped you would all four be going this year.'

In the letter of 22 March, Joe, feeling guilty about letting Decie write all the letters, puts his repentance into practice and writes special bits to each of his sons. To John he describes an unusual operation he has done at Gahini. To David he writes of boats, hunting and painting. Robin gets praise for all he is doing with the CICCU and is encouraged not to mind when people criticize the revival with its teaching on repentance and brokenness. To Michael he writes about birds he has seen and about the possibility of confirmation.

In the 26 April letter, Joe writes that a Belgian annual report described the rebuilding of the hospital as 'excellent, and for very reasonable cost'. He goes on, 'I am glad David's and my efforts have turned out to the glory of God, because there were many anxious moments, strikes etc. Do you remember, David, the two negro spirituals we thought of having written up over the building: "My Lord, what a morning!" and "Nobody knows the trouble I've seen"'. He talks of the Gahini pets as well, especially Chicky the crested crane who followed Janine round the garden and danced with his mate on the lawn, bringing friends and relations, and at night would circle the house and settle on the roof while the wild ones went elsewhere to roost.

There follows a gap in the correspondence to Michael because this was the summer of his one visit to Gahini. It was a poignant time and he remembers 'joyful memories of wind in sails, magical reflections, misty mornings, fishing, story telling by firelight'. There were vivid memories too of 'sweet and painful adolescence and hot lazy days on the lake with

Uncle Bill's family and Janine', and of 'adolescent awk-
wardness with Mum and Dad. By now I knew them less and
less, but this was a brief respite in that painful separation'.

The summer over, Michael returned to England for
school. Joe and Decie worked on. In September, the third
Kabale convention drew many thousands once again. In
November 35 adults and 4 children came for mission and
church committees and stayed for a week, scattered in various houses on Gahini hill. On Christmas day Joe wrote a
long letter, full of memories, saying how they were tempted
to worry about the boys, but 'have peace again, knowing
that you belong, each one of you, to one who can look after
you much much better than ever we can'. In January they
were at Maseno in Uganda, where great crowds gathered
for a large convention. Joe, William and others spoke, and
many came to faith in Jesus Christ. On the same trip they
took Janine to Limuru, a school for expatriate girls near
Nairobi, where she was starting to board. Protected with
barbed wire as it was after Mau Mau, it seemed like a
prison. There were brief respites – visits to Aunt Vera on her
coffee plantation, Girl Guides, Sea Rangers, even visits to
the dentist – but the endless separation from parents and
from home, the waste of precious childhood, was hard.

In the summer of 1956 it was Robin's turn to visit Gahini
before starting at Bart's, his airfares provided for by Granny
Tracey's will. Joe and Decie took Robin with them on a
several-thousand-mile round trip visiting and encouraging
various groups in Tanganyika, Nyasaland, Rhodesia and
the Congo. It was an exciting trip. Once, crossing
Tanganyika, a huge bushfire came sweeping towards them,
doubly alarming as they had extra petrol on the roof in a
leaking tank. They managed to back away to a clearing
when miraculously the wind changed and the fire moved to
one side, giving them a moment to rush past. Yosiya Kinuka
was with them on the trip, but in contrast with Uganda,

where he was accepted as an equal, he experienced increasing discrimination in hotels and restaurants so that he could neither eat nor sleep under the same roof as his brother Christians. Joe, ever the idealist, was pitting his vision of brotherhood prematurely against the social system of the time, and it caused problems.

In October, back at Gahini, Joe was building a new *kazu*. This was a prayer hut, thatched with reedlike *inkenke* grass, similar to the one-or-two-people huts built by some of the hospital staff workers in the 1930s, but able to take a dozen people or more. Christians would gather there – black and white – to study the Bible and to share, discuss and pray informally and at a deep level: a very important aspect of the fellowship at Gahini. It was an appropriate way to do things for at least two reasons: first, it followed the traditional pattern of African decision making, the small local group; and second, in the round building, there was no white missionary standing at the front teaching. Rather, fellow believers gathered round a problem or a need, seeking the help of the Holy Spirit to find the solution and the 'Highest' way forward.

At Christmas, Joe wrote to the boys, 'We do thank God continually for the way he has helped you all and made you all so willing to let us go on with the work he has called us to do of preaching the gospel in Africa.' And Decie in the same letter describes the scene: 'It is Sunday evening after tea, on a brilliant sunny day, and I am sitting typing this on the terrace. The grass lawns are beautifully green and the flower beds are filled with colour. I have just looked up and see our big boat out in the middle of the lake. All of Bill's family and Janine have gone down there for a Sunday evening hymn sing and talk, and some of the visitors have joined them too. . .' Bill and Janet left Gahini for good in February 1957 to continue the education of their five children in England, so Joe had full responsibility for the hospital work again.

On 10 June, shortly before Decie flew back to England for a visit, Joe wrote another important letter to his sons which is worth quoting at some length (the Ridlands Cottage Trust had been wound up and the house handed over to Aunt Christine (Wizz). Joe had not been consulted and was not totally happy about the decision):

So there it is and I am very glad and thankful that all four of you have been so unselfish about it, because it is depriving you all of your last little bit of home in one way. It was partly because of that that I felt it was right for Mum to come home this year and I am sure it is guided. [Then discussing how long Decie can stay.] Gahini is a very big job these days for me. I am back at full general hospital work with the possibility of any sort of operation turning up at any time, not to mention large sums of money to handle all the time as the station grows and our people have bicycles and even cars. Also I am back again as Rural Dean of the Gahini church now that Kosiya Shalita has been made a bishop. Yosiya is with me but there is a great deal of work as you know. Mum is the one who really makes all this job possible. So it is very hard for her to be spared from the work at Gahini. Mum and I need each other more now than ever in our lives together. Some husbands and wives seem to like to have a change – not so us!

In November 1957 Joe and Decie's hard work was recognized by a decoration from King Baudouin of the Belgians: the 'medaille d'or de l'ordre royal du Lion'. From May 1958 till April 1959 the family were together in the Barhams' home at Herne Hill in London. Pam Greaves was with them. (She had joined the Ruanda Mission in 1949 as a secretary, and from 1954 lived with Joe and Decie, helping Joe with secretarial work and his writing, and a valued companion to Decie.) Janine flew to join them in her school holidays for John's marriage to Rhoda Biffen in July 1958.

David married Judith Bell near Oxford in March 1959, Joe returning from a tour of Brazil with Roy Hession two days before the wedding. In August 1959 Joe reached the age of sixty. Back at Gahini now, he wrote, 'I've been trying to realize what it is like to be sixty! I changed into my old Emmanuel hockey shorts and gym shoes this morning and I felt just the same, but I kept asking myself "Am I really sixty?" The Africans are beginning to call me *Umusaza* – "old man".'

Joe might have felt just the same, it may have seemed that Ruanda felt just the same, but like a tiny cloud suddenly looming large, grim changes were on the way.

16

1959–1961: The First Wave of Conflict

In the 1950s, the apparently peaceful, stable and pastoral country of Ruanda, known by the Belgians as 'Le paradis du Congo', began to destabilize. The reasons for this were complex, compounded of tribal history, colonial methods and the 'wind of change' that was beginning to sweep through Africa. For years the Belgian colonial power had used the Tutsi ruling minority to control the country indirectly, exacerbating differences between them and the Hutu in the process. Gradually the more educated of the majority Hutu began to realize that this situation need not continue, and began to stir up dissatisfaction. The Belgians, anxious to avoid the kind of trouble they had experienced in the Congo, began to encourage the Hutus and limit the powers of the Tutsis, for example, by issuing a decree that all chiefs must be elected. Eventually the whole system of government was changed. Instead of the traditional feudal structure of authority, with democracy working at local level through the local chief and his *inama* (council), a Western-style system of one man, one vote was introduced, which inevitably transferred power into the hands of the Hutus, who outnumbered the Tutsis by seven to one.

On 25 July 1959, the King of Ruanda, the Mwami Charles Mutara III Rudahigwa, died suddenly and in mysterious circumstances. His death was recorded in *Ruanda*

Notes, with the comment that 'The Mwami has maintained a most cordial relationship with the Mission, and has graciously visited many of the mission stations; recently he laid the foundation stone of the new school buildings at Gahini.' He was succeeded by the uncrowned Kigeri, aged 24, who also visited Gahini and was given a big welcome there in August. This is how Decie described the events in a letter dated 25 August 1959:

> The country has been very unsettled especially since the king died. There have been many rumours going round . . . On the other hand there has been a great welcome for the new king. He has been on tour all round the country to show himself to his people, and he came here on the 14th in the evening. Dad did a lot to prepare for his visit, with the flags out and a welcome banner out across the road, and we prepared drinks and biscuits for a reception on our veranda. He turned up at 5.30 with a whole convoy of cars, his Belgian adviser, our local administrator and a few soldiers with drums in a lorry behind. They came and sat on our veranda, and then the crowds just swarmed all over our garden trying to get a view of the king . . . Dad read a little speech of welcome and a choir sang two songs, and they made a presentation of a bead-covered spear and stick. He gave a few words, and then they went off up to see the hospital. Actually Dad took him up the hill to see our Chief Kalisa, who is very ill with heart failure. Dad has been going up to see him every day . . .

Mutara's death left the people of Ruanda unsettled and restless, and by the autumn various political parties were becoming more and more active, and dangerous incidents were beginning to flare up. On 7 November, the Governor decided to place the country under martial law, as incendiarism, killings and lawlessness were increasing. Low-flying planes dropped leaflets over Gahini and other places, and schoolboys rushed to get them. Rumours were rife. As *Ruanda Notes* commented, 'Civil war had descended on peaceful Ruanda like a cloud, almost overnight, and no one seemed to know where it had come from and why people were fighting.' Ruanda hit the world news, but Decie in letters home commented that the situation was being misrepresented as a simple uprising of Bahutu against Batutsi, whereas it was more complex, centring in a rapid rise of political parties, possibly stirred up by outside influence. One clear goal seemed to be the dislodging of the Batutsi (now being abandoned by the Belgians in a political volte-face) by force from their dominant position as chiefs and royal counsellors. It was a young Belgian soldier who said to Joe that their job was to push through social and political change as fast as possible and where there was trouble, to 'shoot the tall ones'. But as Bishop Brazier, the Anglican Bishop of Ruanda-Urundi, rightly foresaw, 'This violence and bloodshed will embitter personal relationships for many years to come.'

There were hut-burnings and killings at Shyira and Shyogwe, the latter very near to the royal palace at Nyanza, and groups of Tutsi refugees began to leave, some to be given temporary shelter by the Ruanda Mission at Kabale,

Uganda. Wherever they were, the missionaries did all they could to support and help those in need, regardless of faction or race. Joe's hope was that Gahini would be a safe haven, 'where all could come and take refuge and find the only way of peace, in Jesus'. In November 1959 he wrote that 'some weak Christians were forced to join the gangs under threats of reprisals, but the *Balokole* everywhere stood firm and gave grand witness'. At Gahini things remained calm for a while, and Joe described in *Ruanda Notes* how, when trouble-making gangs were expected, Bahutu and Batutsi around Gahini remained united, requesting government troops to stay away. He went on, 'The Communion Service on Sunday, 15 November had special meaning for us as we knelt side by side, Bahutu and Batutsi, black and white, to thank God for the Blood of Jesus shed to make all men one. However, as violence flared up repeatedly all over the country, it seemed to Bishop Brazier that the troubles were affecting fellowship among Christians: 'There are very few who are not partisan at heart and this does affect spiritual life. It means that there is not the "walking in the light" that there used to be. We are more accommodating in church councils because everyone is careful not to stir up trouble. The undercurrent of distrust and suspicion is always there.'

In October 1959 Joe and Decie's son John arrived with his wife Rhoda to join the hospital team at Gahini, setting Joe free to travel again. In February 1960 Joe spoke at the Congo Protestant Council conference, and Decie wrote that 'some of the missions are planning to hand over their stations and houses and all management to the Africans at Congo independence in June'. She went on, 'We don't know at all how things are going to go here in Ruanda. There are a lot of changes preparatory to the elections in June. Many of the *sous-chefs* have been dismissed (including our two local keen Protestants) and three *sous-chefferies* grouped into one new "commune" with a burgomaster! Rumours still go on, and there is no trust in the country . . .'

In June 1960 Decie wrote:

We shall not be coming to England in September – we do feel now that Dad, with all his experience and spiritual vision, is needed out here in this troubled country. The authorities are convinced that the Batutsi element – particularly one political party, UNAR, is staging a rising. They are also convinced that we, as a mission, are UNAR supporters, and dreadful things are being said about us. Actually as regards political parties we are neutral, as a mission, and in fact are friends of the Banyaruanda whoever comes to us. Dad has come in very effectively on several situations which might have blown up – even here on this station among our own people. In the last few days we have had news trickling through of destroying bands on the move again in the Kigali area, and many say it is only a matter of time before they come here.

In November, at the time of the appointment of Gregoire Kayibanda as head of state, Decie described how Ephraim Muneyi, former headmaster of Gahini school, and now church treasurer and secretary, was seized by police, beaten up and taken to prison where he spent the night and was beaten again, as were two Gahini schoolmasters on the same day. She commented, 'Justice is dead in this country, it just makes us all so sad.'

And again she wrote in June 1961:

We had rather a terrific week last week in many ways, mostly arising from the fact that the present authorities in power are throwing their weight about. There has been quite a lot of banditry round here, and even three houses in Gahini out at the back were hit about. Many people have been beaten up, including Yohana Gasega, the old hereditary chief on this hill.

On one hill at least, people were being beaten up until they cursed the Mwami and agreed to join the party in power. Ephraim Muneyi was threatened in his house and he spent one night with us, until Dad got a police guard for his house.

In June too Michael, aged twenty-one and just finished at Cambridge, came out with a friend for his second and last visit to Gahini since he left Africa nine years before – a brief interlude before the old order in Ruanda and at Gahini finally collapsed. The newly elected local burgomasters had voted to abolish the monarchy and to set up a Republic with an elected President, a decision which was confirmed by a UNO-controlled referendum and which led to the new outburst of violence. Elections in September, based on the new system of 'one man, one vote' returned a large Hutu majority. Suddenly, in September the storm broke at Gahini, where slanderous reports were still circulating linking Joe with the main Tutsi political party. The story was told in *Ruanda Notes* mostly in letters from Joe, himself suddenly 'a refugee' in Fort Portal, Toro, Uganda. In a letter dated 9 September 1961, he wrote:

For nearly two years we have been living and carrying on in Ruanda under a state of martial law; it has been a strain but also a privilege to be with, and to suffer with, our beloved Ruanda in its time of need. But as passions have been aroused (stirred, we believe, by the evil one) a few have become our enemies. We have had to ... stand out against cruelty and persecution. But the pattern of the elimination of the Batutsi and of the members of the monarchist party has gone on systematically and relentlessly, leaving a mounting number of refugees, and scars that will take years to heal.

... Sometimes one has to act quickly without thought of consequences. For example, a year ago the *Mugabikazi* (mother of the King) arrived for treatment at Gahini. While she was with us her home and property were destroyed, and her cattle killed and stolen, so she turned to us for protection. For nine months this dignified lady was our guest. Later, with the Belgian Government's permission, I took the *Mugabikazi* into Uganda for refuge. But this, and a number of other instances, have drawn the fire on Gahini and on me personally. I have protested my neutrality as a doctor and as a preacher of the gospel, and our non-participation in politics. As Gahini has continued to seek reconciliation and peace we have been accused of holding up the trend of the country.

The Queen Mother suffered from two distinct medical conditions, fibroids and asthma. On 10 May 1961, Decie had written home to Michael that they had been to Mbarara, 'taking Kigeri's mother on her way towards Kampala where we want her to see a specialist about her condition. People are saying we helped her to escape from Ruanda, but this is a genuine case of illness'. John Church recalls:

My father was by nature a royalist, seeing the monarchy as the epitome of all that is good in national cohesion. He had become friendly with the Ruandan royal family. He was other-worldly and didn't see the political undercurrents . . . I remember vividly two further visits which Kigeri, still uncrowned and now without Belgian advisers, made to Gahini. On one occasion people came running from the hills as the drums rose to a crescendo. Then there was silence. You could have heard a pin drop as Kigeri spoke peace to his people. Next came the response: first a lone voice, then the singing and the drums joining in – an electrifying and unforgettable moment. On the second occasion he arrived at Gahini with a huge cavalcade of limousines. As coffee and biscuits were served, he asked for a private audience with my father and me. His request was for me to be his personal medical adviser. The Belgians, now strongly pro-Hutu, were refusing him all advice, including medical advice, so he was turning to me because I was neither Belgian nor Roman Catholic. It was a very difficult situation. What could I say but that I was honoured and would be happy to do so, within the limitations of the hospital, but that no political significance should be read into my agreement. This was how the Queen Mother came to us for treatment.

It was not long afterwards, just before the referendum on the monarchy, that the Belgians bundled Kigeri into a plane and banished him to Tanzania. Dramatically, on the eve of the referendum his supporters brought him back over the border in a canoe, then drove him past all barriers disguised as a small-pox patient in an ambulance so that as the polling booths opened, he appeared in his royal regalia in the centre of Kigali. At the other end of the lake, at Gahini, the drums were rumbling from hill to hill: 'The King is back in Kigali!' Shortly afterwards, a new message: 'The King is dead!' This was incorrect. In fact he had been sent back to Tanzania.

There could be said to have been a trinity at the heart of Ruanda: the King, the Queen Mother, and the Royal Drum. This sacred drum *Kalinga* symbolized the authority of the King. At the time when the Queen Mother came to Gahini for treatment, her son by now banished, the drum was brought in a huge box 6 foot square, and ceremoniously lifted onto Joe's veranda where it stayed. The king's palace was no longer se-cure, and the Batutsi reckoned that Gahini was neutral ground, and the safest place for it to be. One Sunday after-noon, as we were enjoying tea overlooking the lake, sounds of turmoil were heard from the hospital. I rushed up in my car to find a murderous gang attacking the house where the Queen Mother, now back from Kampala, was staying. Somehow the gang were calmed and persuaded to go away. I returned to the house to find her surrounded by twelve fully armed men, guarding her. However she could not stay, and at 2 a.m., brav-ing the curfew and covered in blankets, she was walked to the foot of the hill where a vehicle with no lights was waiting and she was driven to safety in Uganda. Thus her life was saved. As soon as possible, the Drum had to go too. It was no suitable lodger for a mission veranda.

To Joe, all this was exciting stuff, but it was a death blow to his future in Ruanda. It was naïve to suppose that, having given refuge to two of the symbols of royal power, he could continue to live and work as an unmarked and neutral doctor in the current state of unrest. Twice he was warned, by faithful African friends, that he was on the blacklist and his life was in danger. Returning from a big Christian convention in Kenya in August 1961, Joe found an urgent letter waiting from Godfrey Hindley, Secretary of the Mission, telling him to go at once to Urundi to see him. Joe recalled:

I went with my wife and passed through marauding bands around Nyanza. After supper, Godfrey broke the news that Mr Murray, the senior British Consul in Ruanda, had advised me to leave Ruanda temporarily for two reasons: in view of the extent to which I have 'become a centre of political controversy in the Gahini area', and because he had fears for my safety. He had added to Godfrey that if I refused he would instruct the Foreign Office to remove me. Ken Moynagh had come up from Matana to be with me. They were both emphatic that I must not refuse. We talked and prayed till midnight.

I would never have left Gahini at this time of worst testing and threatened attack, unless I had been ordered to go. But somehow I have a feeling that God is behind this move, so we are resting in him and going on a step at a time . . . On Thursday August 31st we left, leaving our house looking as normal as possible. Our tear-off calendar had this text for the last morning: 'The Lord was with Joseph'. So I (Joe) took it as my promise!

As John, who stayed behind, commented, 'Instead of a proper wonderful farewell to celebrate a lifetime given to Ruanda, they were bundled unceremoniously into a car with no one knowing.' John stayed on with his wife Rhoda and their baby Jonathan, but soon, in early September, there were rumours of an impending attack on Gahini. On 12 September, despite reassurances from the senior Belgian army commander in Ruanda that all would be well, looking through his binoculars John saw plumes of smoke progressing some 20 miles away. Tutsi homesteads were being systematically set on fire. By the next day, gangs with pangas had reached the adjacent hill. John called a prayer meeting of senior missionaries – there was no human protection against the impending holocaust. Every homestead was set alight, up to that of their nearest neighbours, so much so that cinders from the next house were blowing on John and Rhoda's home, but neither the hospital, nor their home, nor that of any other mission workers, were attacked. At midnight that night, John typed a letter for *Ruanda Notes* beginning, 'This is the saddest letter I could ever have to write to you. It all came like a sudden whirlwind – today!' He went on to recount how as he was doing the ward round, suddenly a tall Mututsi, exhausted, rushed into the ward, pursued by a Hutu gang, and grasped John by the ankles crying 'Save me!' Once again death stared John in the face. Enraged that this mob should invade the neutrality of the hospital – a sanctuary where he was striving to save life, John drove them all out, swinging his stethoscope, his only 'weapon', furiously at them. He took the quivering man into the prayer room – the spiritual heart of the hospital – and under the symbol of the open Bible above the front door, he calmed the frenzied group, sat them on the grass and tried to reason with them. The exhausted man was taken away later by Belgian soldiers. Later that evening John walked alone down the central avenue of trees lovingly planted by Joe. The whole place was ablaze, and so bright one could almost have read a newspaper in the glare. Clearly he sensed Someone walking alongside, and was comforted – there was peace in the eye of the storm.

Over the next few days three thousand people and a thousand long-horned cattle arrived for refuge. Within a very short time the cows had demolished everything – the place was a desert. The cows began to die and the refugees survived by eating them, leaving two thousand horns. The situation was desperate. But there were miracles, like 'Doc', the intrepid missionary engineer in Kenya who received a clear call from God in a vision, to sell all he had, buy the biggest ranch wagon he could and drive west. Arriving at the Congo border, he was thwarted in his westward progress at gunpoint, so went back to Kabale in south-west Uganda where someone ran up with a note from John at Gahini: 'Please help – we need transport!' At once he turned south and reaching Gahini, began regularly to go out ahead of the gangs and rescue whoever he could. All those rescued were given refuge at Gahini – and food, which Doc bought in by the ton from the local markets. They were then driven in trucks to safety in Uganda. His work done, Doc left as mysteriously as he had arrived.

This, the first of successive waves of conflict in Ruanda, caused millions to leave their homes. It was as he pastored refugees at one of the camps at Nyamata that Yona Kanamuzeyi, a pastor who had been touched by the revival many years before, was executed without trial in 1964, accused of 'standing for the word of God and for loving everyone indiscriminately'. His reply when told of this accusation was, 'These two things, the word of God and the love of God are like garments with which God has clothed me, and I cannot go about without them.' He loved and ministered to Hutu and Tutsi alike. On 23 January 1964 this loved and respected pastor was arrested, taken from his home and shot on the bridge at Nyamata and his body was thrown in the river. He is commemorated in the Memorial Chapel of St Paul's Cathedral as a modern martyr, and in a book which Joe Church and others wrote about him called *Forgive Them*.

Ruanda attained independence in July 1962. John hoped to continue running the hospital and had great plans for developing it and increasing the staff. Over the four years that he worked in Ruanda, moving backwards and forwards between Gahini and Kigeme, he was the only doctor in his hospital. Not once did he share a ward round with a professional colleague. One night, delayed until after curfew, he, Rhoda and baby Jonathan were brought to a sudden halt in their car by a 30-foot log across the road. Guns were thrust in through the windows. 'I'm your doctor,' John said, in Lunyaruanda, 'Is there anything I can do?' Mollified, the gangs allowed them to pass. But there was no future for them in the newly independent country now known as Rwanda. The hospital was boycotted by the Republican régime, who threatened that anyone entering would be shot. John had promised to be the King's physician and so, like his father, he was a marked man. He could no longer practise. It was time to go.

After a visit to the UK, he and Rhoda returned not to Rwanda, but to Uganda, where over the next ten years John played a part in the training of a thousand doctors both at Makerere Medical School and later in Nairobi, Kenya. For Joe and Decie too, God had important new work for them to do.

17

1961–1972: New Work for God in Uganda

Crossing the border into Uganda, their American Ford station wagon packed to the roof, Joe, Decie, Mike and his friend and Janine headed for Kabarole in Fort Portal, where Joe had been invited some time before to reorganize and rebuild the old CMS hospital, originally established by Dr Albert Cook. Joe was sixty-two and near retirement, but God still had work for them to do. In Uganda the 'wind of change' was blowing strongly. Independence was just over a year away. They settled into an empty CMS mission house with hardly any furniture and were deeply touched when word got round and every day groups of Africans came with gifts of food. God was providing for them as he had provided for Elijah long ago.

Writing in the *Ruanda Notes* review for 1961–62, Joe explained that although building a completely new pioneer hospital somewhere else had been a possibility, the people of Toro had been insistent that their mission hospital with all its old associations should be rebuilt on the old site at Kabarole, the cathedral centre, in Fort Portal, the capital of Toro district in western Uganda. It was a beautiful site looking out towards the snow peaks of the Ruwenzori and facing the high hill of the Mukama's palace. The Mukama, the king of Toro, had been born at the hospital, and on 4 September 1961 it was he who laid the foundation stone and building began. One of the many remarkable things in Joe and Decie's story is the seamless calm with which they appear to have said farewell to Ruanda where so much of their lives had been invested, and almost without looking back, moved on to the next task. God's timing was astonishing, and so was their trust in him. The building of the new hospital began four days after their unplanned departure from Gahini.

Decie's letters to England at this time show calm acceptance too, mixed with deep concern for their Ruandan friends. On 16 October they drove to Shyogwe, Ruanda, for an emergency mission meeting. They heard many moving stories, like that of a young Christian teacher, shot in his house as he sat preparing his lessons, who had testified courageously in his last few moments that his home was not here but in heaven. On the way back they stayed for a night with fellow missionaries, the Sisleys, at Gahini and found it overflowing with several hundred refugees and their cattle. Decie wrote:

> I can hardly begin to tell you all the sad stories there are of the events of the last five or six weeks . . . Men were tied up and thrown into the lake. Two women drowned themselves in the lake after their men had been killed . . . There were at least 30 murders on one hill alone. There seemed a sinister and sad atmosphere over the whole country as we drove through. The evil is still going on unchecked, and over 18,500 are registered as refugees now in Uganda, with many more unregistered.

Once or twice they came across old Gahini employees who had travelled the long journey to safety in Uganda, and when possible they gave them employment in their new home. They visited the refugee camps too, and at the

Rukinga Valley camp found many of their old friends from Gahini, with Yosiya Kinuka ministering faithfully to his former parishioners there.

On Boxing Day they returned briefly to Gahini as John and Rhoda's guests, sitting down to their traditional Gahini goose Christmas supper with Janine who had now left school, David and his wife Judy, now living in Nairobi, and several missionaries. After finally clearing and packing up their old house they returned (surviving a near-fatal brake failure halfway across Uganda) to Toro: 'With a growing certainty that our time at Gahini was over and that the Lord wanted us in Toro, it was easier to have his peace.' They were sad though to see John struggling with an almost impossible situation. Not only was his own continuing work at Gahini under threat, but the new minister for health was determined to dismiss all Batutsi medical staff from Ruanda hospitals – by far the majority of all trained staff.

In October 1962 Uganda celebrated Independence with a service in the cathedral at Kampala and an official ceremony of lowering and raising the flags together with a tattoo and fireworks display.

Janine had left Limuru and for nine months in 1962 she lived with her parents at Fort Portal. It was a happy time for them all. They had a lovely house, Decie had far fewer responsibilities than in Ruanda, and they were able to relax and do things together. Janine joined her father playing golf, and with Decie she sang the *Messiah* in the cathedral and went to music appreciation classes run by the British Council on Government Hill. Then she headed for London to study physiotherapy. Robin, now married to Joan, and Michael were following the pattern set by Joe and then John, studying medicine at Emmanuel College, Cambridge and then at Bart's before starting to practise. Joe was thrilled to think of Michael at Bart's, writing, 'Are you doing any small-bore shooting? Have a shoot for the Lady

Ludlow cup – as I did! How is the C.U. [Christian Union] going? Are you still president? That's more than I was. I was secretary and captain of the hockey team, but I would put the C.U. before that.' Decie seemed wonderfully well able to 'let her children go' – no doubt because she trusted God to look after them. She and Joe were not present at Robin's wedding to Bart's nurse Joan Bee, herself the daughter of pioneer missionaries, in June 1961, and Decie wrote at the time, 'It is sad for us not to be there, but it can't always be for families to be together, especially when living so far away. Dad had none of his relatives at our wedding, and I had just Aunt Vee, as it was at Namirembe.' On Robin's wedding day, 'Dad put the framed portraits of Robin and Joan and the wedding invitation on a small table in the centre of the sitting room . . . so we were reminded of them, and you all that were gathered there, constantly, all through that day. How much we should have loved to be there!' Similarly they could not be at Michael's wedding in June 1965 to Bart's nurse Anne Butler at Pyrford where Howard and Lizzo now lived.

About Janine too, on her own in London, but also based at Pyrford at weekends, Decie seems remarkably calm, relying on the boys to keep an eye on her but allowing herself to query gently the mention of a 'cocktail party' and to wonder whether the 'distracting things of the world' were ensnaring her a bit. Although Joe and Decie and their children sacrificed a very great deal of normal family life to the demands of Joe's calling, it is impressive that within a few years, once their studies were finished, all five of Joe and Decie's children would be back working in Africa. Three would be doctors, one an architect, and all would be living and working as committed Christians.

John, having hoped to continue Joe's work at Gahini, went on to lecture and do research at Makerere University Medical School and then to work for several years in orthopaedics at the Kenyatta teaching hospital, Nairobi. As he wrote, 'Africa is a more needy place than ever, but a new Africa is emerging which is quite different from the old. The younger generation is largely materialist, nationalist and godless, but it is a great privilege to be able to help in some small way.' David became a partner with Hughes and Polkinghorne, one of the main architectural practices in Uganda, working long hours and rejoicing in combining his knowledge of local building methods gained at Gahini with his knowledge of modern design learnt at architectural school in Oxford. Robin came out with the Ruanda Mission in 1963, seconded to the Church of Uganda to build up a medical team and reopen Kabarole Hospital with the specific aim of showing God's love through healing. The logo of the hospital, a red cross over the Christian cross, indicated healing of body and of soul. And Michael worked for many years with Save the Children in Uganda, making a big impact on child health by setting up local clinics and giving basic health education to mothers. All four were gifted in many directions and had many interests, often playing the guitar and singing barber-shop together at Christian gatherings, keen on sport, and loving boats and the water. Janine too came back to Africa, married to Dr Hugh Coleridge who became a Government hospital doctor in Uganda. To all of them, Africa was home.

In 1964 Joe and Decie officially retired as Joe reached 65. The job of rebuilding the Fort Portal hospital was done, and it was to be officially opened by Princess Margaret in March the following year, when Robin and Joe showed her round, glad to have a moment to tell her of the special spiritual calling of the hospital. Meanwhile, Joe and Decie went back to England for six months, and for some of the time were lent a flat near St Mary's Hospital, Paddington, where Janine was studying physiotherapy, and were thrilled to be able to have both Janine and Michael with them there. Once Joe, with

Michael's help, had attended to his first priority of obtaining a good open car to rush around in, they took part in many Christian gatherings around the country. Notable among them was a visit with Festo Kivengere to Cambridge and the CICCU when there were many conversions among the students. This was also Joe's farewell visit to Cambridge as the CICCU's 'own missionary' which he had been for the last 37 years. Once again he thanked God for the incalculable effect that the faithful prayers of the CICCU had had in East Africa as God worked in revival. They had fun too sailing on the Broads and in the Solent, and visiting the Traceys in Devon – happy times in a perfect English summer.

They didn't stay in England though. Despite Joe's retirement, yet another plan was afoot – to go back to Uganda, but this time to Kampala, where they would eventually act as wardens for a new venture to which Corrie ten Boom was giving much support (a Dutch Christian who was sent to Ravensbruck concentration camp for sheltering Jews, but

survived and became a well-known writer and speaker) –
the Lweza conference centre off the Kampala-Entebbe
road. But first, most of it would have to be built, with design
help from David and under Joe's supervision. Joe described
the new project in his 1965 Christmas circular letter:

> You may remember that my wife and I came back to Uganda to
> retire just a year ago. We felt that this was a definite call from
> God. Harry and Evelyn Campbell had invited us to come and
> help them in the developing of their home and grounds as a
> Christian conference centre. There is a real need of a place of
> retreat such as this in the centre of Uganda, where people can
> come apart for rest and prayer and for the deepening of spiri-
> tual life. I am glad to be back at my old hobby of building and
> creating, which is so satisfying when so much that is going on
> in the world at this time is destructive. Decie too finds much
> joy in the flower and vegetable gardens. Our home, to be called
> the Warden's House, is nearly completed.
>
> One of our visions for 'Lweza' was that friends on world
> travel could drop down out of the skies and visit us, as we are
> only thirteen miles from the international airport at Entebbe
> on Lake Victoria. We have dammed up a stream down in the
> forest below us, and we send our guests down to see the mon-
> keys, the hornbills, the grey and red parrots and the long-tailed
> butterflies and to see how the ram water pump is working.

Sadly, although the Lweza centre was a success as a centre
of revival, there were misunderstandings which left Joe
saddened and bewildered. He and Decie moved to 202,
Sentema Road, Mengo, a rented house behind Namirembe
Hill, belonging to William Nagenda, and next door to their
African friend John Wilson. Their hope was to live out the
rest of their lives in Africa. In many ways this was a good
time for them, in Kampala. There in the historic Christian
centre many people came to see them – old friends and

young from the *Balokole*. It was while they were living here that Joe was approached about writing his account of the revival movement and did much of the research and the writing. Yet again Decie created a beautiful garden, and Joe resurrected the public tennis court near the Cathedral, using crushed ant-heap for the finished surface.

The year 1966 heralded a time of change and distress in Uganda. The President, Milton Obote, used a tough soldier and his troops to help him subdue the Kabaka of Buganda, whose province was threatening to secede from Uganda. The President was successful. The Kabaka fled to Britain where he died three years later. The soldier's name was Idi Amin. Five years later in 1971, the corruption and oppression of Obote's regime had led to such unpopularity that the military coup which brought Amin into power was welcomed at first. David Church remembers the moment of the coup, as their home on Namirembe Hill overlooked Kampala city:

> Bursts of gunfire in the night sounded at first like firework celebrations. Then throughout the next morning from our vantage point on the hill we could follow with binoculars the progress of the battle from one strategic site to another. Then silence. No traffic. Only the sound of birds in the eucalyptus trees. Then the crackling report on the radio announced that Idi Amin had taken control, and a murmuring in the valley rapidly turned into a babble of sound as people took to the streets in celebration, many crowding into overloaded lorries waving branches and singing. Amin's style seemed less pompous than Obote's – he drove his own jeep instead of being driven in a Mercedes with outriders. He started with a popular move – bringing the Kabaka's body back to Uganda for burial – but slowly the country degenerated into anarchy with raiding gangs at large, and Amin the efficient jovial soldier gave way to Amin Dada the tyrant. The rest is history.

Many of Amin's worst atrocities were directed against Christians, but as with Mau Mau in Kenya, they had been prepared by God's work of revival. With shining faith, thousands faced torture and death undaunted, notable among them the loved and respected Archbishop Janani Luwum, who was converted through the ministry of two *balokole* in 1948 and murdered by Amin in 1977.

By 1972 many missionaries had left. Erica Sabiti, archbishop of Uganda, Rwanda and Burundi since 1966, had encouraged them to stay in a new supportive role and many, Joe and Decie among them, had done so. But law and order were breaking down in Uganda. Gangs of thugs were going around with battering rams breaking into houses. Security had to become tighter and tighter and Joe became tense and worried by it all, sleeping with the house keys under his pillow. Some of the *balokole* too were becoming very legalistic. They criticized Joe for ridiculous things – for having a small Cairn terrier for protection and not simply trusting the Lord; or for wearing a moustache which they saw as wanting to appear macho. At last Joe and Decie were persuaded that the time had come for them to settle in England. All their four sons and their families had now left, and only Janine and Hugh were still in Uganda, where Hugh was medical officer in charge of the Mbarara government hospital. Joe and Decie flew back in June – they were all packed up just as Amin threw the Asians out. Once again they got out just in time, and Joe commented on how God seemed to have taken them away from all that was about to befall Uganda, much as he removed them from Ruanda 11 years earlier some 10 days before the villages went up in smoke around Gahini.

Joe had given 44 years of his life to Africa. He had remained within the fold of the Anglican Church, with which he always seemed to have a relationship rather like that of an impatient adolescent with its parents. As he and his fellow believers black and white continued their work, scattered over a huge area of East Africa and in other parts of the world too, a sleepy, hypocritical, unenthusiastic and often sinful church was transformed into a shining, vibrant and witnessing community. How was this done? What were Joe's particular gifts and characteristics that helped it to happen? And what, if any, special methods did he use?

His most important tool was Bible-based preaching: preaching of redemption through the blood of Jesus shed on the cross. His strong emphasis on the Bible was also essential in discerning when false doctrine or various excesses were mixing with the fervour of the revival. Frequently Joe and Lawrence Barham would examine the Scriptures with the African Christians, and would gently but firmly make it clear from the word of God if they were going down the wrong path.

We have seen already that Joe was not considered to be an outstanding preacher. We have seen too how he supplemented his own limitations – for example poor linguistic ability – by working with a team. One remarkable feature of Joe's preaching was his use of pictorial images – something which appealed immediately to his African hearers. There were several of these pictures, and they were used many times so that they became almost icons of the revival. The pin-men pictures have been mentioned already. Later, arising directly from the 'bowed neck' dream of Kilimenti Semugabo, came the 'bowed neck' motto cards which became basic doctrinal visual aids. In the first, *The Secret of Revival*, a man stands stiff-necked before Christ. Then the 'I' bows and forms the 'C' of Christ. In the second card, *The Secret of Fellowship*, two men with stiff necks grow further and further apart until they turn and ask forgiveness; then they kneel at the cross, their arms forming a 'V' for Victory as they shake hands – two I's in harmony. One source of inspiration for this card was a model plane made by Michael as a boy, with the V-sign on its cockpit cover. The third card, *The Secret of Prayer*, shows the same two reconciled people beginning to pray and to work together for revival.

This reminds us that another essential element of Joe's work for God was prayer – the victorious, effective prayer of people in fellowship with God and with each other. This was the prayer of the *kazu* or prayer hut, the prayer of the fellowship group. It was also the earnest prayer of the individual who drew apart to spend time with God. The story is told for instance of Joe out on medical safari, when people would queue up early outside his tent, waiting for treatment. 'Don't disturb him,' they would say. 'He is praying. If we disturb him now, we may get the wrong medicine!'

Some of Joe's gifts are easy to see – his energy, his enthusiasm, his wide vision combined with attention to detail. Remarkable too was his ability to cut through the contemporary image of missionaries as people on a pedestal, who didn't allow Africans into their houses. Somehow, without making a political issue of it, he saw them as people just like himself with whom it was important to form a relationship and from whom he could learn. Humility, honesty and a sensitive conscience like his father's all played a part here. He demanded the highest standards of himself and of other people.

Perhaps it was because he was an enthusiast that people tended to react to him in one of two ways. Some were inspired to follow his vision. Notable among these were the dedicated women who worked with him. Eileen Faber, self-assured, talented, an enthusiast in her own right, shared his vision and ran the school at her own expense for several years. Pam Greaves was a quieter personality, but she also worked with Joe as his self-supporting secretary for many years and virtually became a member of the family. She eventually married Roy Hession when his wife Revel died in an accident. Pam had first found reality in her own Christian experience through a visit of the revival team to her church in England in 1947, and this had drawn her to Ruanda. She found Joe easy to work with, with a sense of humour and a very natural way with the Africans. She loved Decie too, 'very different from Joe, but pure gold'. Another supporter was Claire Lise de Benoit. From an aristocratic Swiss family, she adored Joe and shared his spiritual vision. Her family urged Joe to regard their beautiful house overlooking Lake Geneva as home, and Claire Lise, together with Berthe Ryf, became Joe's link with Europe, organizing his visits to Switzerland.

But enthusiasts can make other people irritated and, as we have seen, Joe had this effect on some people, particularly those in authority, who felt threatened by him as he questioned their well-established structures. Even Bert Osborn, a dedicated younger missionary, admitted that 'some of us who held Joe in the highest esteem also experienced some of his exasperating traits. For instance, we respected him immensely for the strength of conviction with which he held certain principles, but he was often very woolly about the way those principles should be put into practice.' This comment may reflect the same characteristic that one of Joe's sons observed in other contexts, that to him the message and the broad picture were the important thing. Detail in some respects did not interest Joe, and Decie would quietly correct him when he got facts wrong. But in practical matters like building, or making a splint for a baby with a club foot, he took endless pains to get every detail right.

Despite his broad interests, regarding the revival Joe was single minded to a fault. This affected his relationship with the wider church, in that he was not always readily able to see that Christians with a different approach to his own might also have some grasp of the truth and something to contribute. It also affected his family, in that he tended to expect of them the same loyalty and dedication that he himself readily gave to God and to his vision of 'the Highest'. And he can't always have been easy to be married to. As one of his sons put it, 'He was a great adventurer – Decie was horrified at some of his impossible ideas and adventures.' On the other hand, he was never dull and always great fun to be with. Energetic, creative, practical, he not only dreamed up exciting projects, but executed them with such hard work and enthusiasm that they persisted. The Walrus cruises continue to this day, combining excellence in sailing instruction with solid Christian teaching. KPS continues as one of Uganda's most sought-after schools.

Some of his missionary colleagues have made comments on his character and methods of work. Wendy Moynagh, for example, first met Joe when he was a medical student helping to lead a beach mission at Southwold in Suffolk and she was a child of eight: 'Lawrence Barham was there too . . . We all thought they were wonderful! And so they were – great fun, overflowing with love towards us children and full of zeal in their witness for Jesus. They made a lasting impression, which has remained all through the years.' Later, Wendy and her husband Kenneth worked in Ruanda and Urundi with the Ruanda Mission, when 'Joe and Decie had an enormous influence on our lives. They were true friends, and always so caring, always ready to help or give advice or to share from their own experiences.' As Wendy remembered too:

Joe's preaching of the gospel was simple and direct. He had a clear message to give and there was no mistaking the truth. He himself seemed to live a transparent life. He set himself the highest standards and made us want to do the same. There was no hypocrisy in Joe. He knew himself to be a sinner saved by the grace of the Lord Jesus Christ and daily cleansed in his blood. This was the central message, and he loved to remind us of the need to hold out our cleansed cups to Jesus to be daily, constantly filled with his Holy Spirit. That is how Joe and Decie lived – their lives were a constant benediction. He was a natural leader, and yet he preferred to be part of a team. He was a true man of God and a faithful messenger of the truth of revival that God had entrusted to him.

Dr Kenneth Buxton commented:

Joe was not a teacher, but he had a great gift of bringing the Bible to life, and applying it to practical living. His great theme was to speak of Jesus – 'Revival is Jesus' – and how in his light we see our sin, our need of repentance and of cleansing in his blood. He cared very much for the message of the cross and was deeply troubled by news of any person or influence which took away from that message and the authority of Scripture. Without being critical he would always seek a way of reconciliation, but without compromise of the truth.

To Ian Leakey, 'First impressions were of a quiet, unassuming, hesitant person with no obvious gifts as a speaker, but one knew immediately that he lived his life in a close, informal, uncomplicated relationship with God. This was quite disarming and a little frightening . . . there was the feeling that there was a secret weapon somewhere. The "secret weapon" was of course the person of the Holy Spirit.' And Dr Harold Adeney remembers Joe and Decie:

Joe was a visionary. When he got carried away with wild ideas, Decie was the one who kept his feet on the ground. It was wonderful staying with them, with breakfast on the veranda and the view over the lake. Joe loved order and beauty, grass cut, paths weeded, trees planted in just the right place. Decie with her green fingers loved and nurtured plants.

Joe pioneered a new relationship between white and black Christians. In the early days, the missionaries had led and the

Africans had followed. Joe saw himself as brother, not *Bwana* [master]: we are all sinners, we all come to Jesus for cleansing, black and white the same. Nonetheless, he was also a man of his time with a public school and university education. There was therefore a natural affinity between him and the Tutsi in Ruanda and their privileged position did not appear to trouble him.

Joe's pioneering in relationships between black and white Christians was instinctive, spiritual and based on the biblical oneness of believers. It was not political. The growing pressure for social change in Ruanda which began in the 1950s was primarily political and, apart from being available to give help to all in need, it was not an issue with which Joe felt called to become involved, or about which he gave specific teaching.

Joe often referred to Lake Mohasi as Ruanda's Sea of Galilee, and he seems to have held a clear vision, particularly after his visit to Israel, of Jesus in the similar hills above Capernaum. Jesus too emphasized the spiritual priority of repentance and faith in his acts of healing. Jesus was surrounded by strong political anti-Roman pressures, but he skilfully avoided these and healed a Roman centurion's servant instead. Some 35 years after Jesus' teaching and death, the political uprisings of that time resulted in the sack of Jerusalem and much bloodshed. Similarly, during the 30 years after Joe and Decie left Ruanda, the pressure was to increase.

18

1972–1997: Before and After the Genocide

With the help of Robin, who had moved there with his family, Joe and Decie settled in the small village of Little Shelford, not far from Cambridge, in 1972. Joe's brother Bill had gone into general practice there on leaving Africa in 1957. Christine (Wizz) also lived nearby in Great Shelford for a while. Joe and Decie's 1972 Christmas letter described the 'exciting experience of settling into life in England': 'Our house is small but easy to run, and stands back in its own plot in the main street of Little Shelford. We are two doors off from my brother Bill's house, and our third son Robin has joined Dr Charles Sergel's practice, and has a house only five minutes walk from here, and we can see the elm trees of their garden. So here we are, learning to manage in England – doing housework, biking to the village shops, making improvements to the house.'

They were also making links with the parish church, with the CICCU in nearby Cambridge, with the Ruanda Mission Council in London and with their large family and with many Christian friends, including visiting Roy Hession and his revival house parties at Southwold in Suffolk each summer. Their priority, and one of Joe's reasons for coming back to England, was to see through publication of first, a revised edition of *Every Man a Bible Student*, and then, his autobiographical history of the East African revival, *Quest for the Highest*. Their annual Christmas letters give high spots of their years. In 1974 they attended the fiftieth jubilee of the Norfolk Broads Walrus cruises which Joe had started. Joe also visited the Leysin revival conference in Switzerland, the twenty-eighth since the first one when Lawrence Barham, Bill Butler and Joe had been invited there from East Africa as a team. In 1976 they joined the Ruanda Mission house party at the Keswick centenary convention. Joe also went to Uganda for the fourth Kabale convention, which were held every ten years. In 1976 the revised edition of *Every Man a Bible Student* was published and went into several reprints. Joe had worked hard for four years on this revision, convinced that individual study and understanding of the Bible was essential to the spiritual well-being of the nation. In 1976 too, Bill Church, whose wife Janet had died of cancer in 1972, married an old friend, Mildred Forder, one-time hospital sister at Gahini. It was also in this year that Joe was diagnosed as having a slow-growing cancer of the prostate, which was controlled with daily hormone tablets. He was also found to have a small duodenal ulcer. The specialist at Addenbrooke's Hospital, finding this, asked Joe if he had a tendency to worry. 'Oh no', Joe replied, convinced that he cast all his anxiety on God. He was surprised, on talking this over with Robin, when Robin pointed out, 'But Dad, of course you have always worried – you are a perfectionist!' Ruefully he recognized that Robin was right.

In 1977 Yosiya Kinuka, 'perhaps my closest African brother', came to England for medical treatment. In 1979 Joe reached eighty and Decie seventy-five. They were both still riding bicycles. Sadly, Bill died that year, having been married to Mildred for only three years. In 1980 Joe and Decie celebrated their golden wedding with a thanksgiving service in the chapel of the CMS headquarters in London. In 1981 *Quest for the Highest* was published. In the foreword, Joe tells the story of its inception:

> There was one place where people used to meet for coffee in the centre of Kampala. It was the tearoom of the CMS bookshop on a wide veranda overlooking the central shopping area. One morning, December 10, 1966, a voice called up to me – it was Professor Noel King, the energetic head of the Religious Studies Department of Makerere University, asking me to come to his office as he had something important he wished to put to me. He asked me if I would be interested in our retirement in Uganda in doing some research into the history of the *Balokole* (revival) movement in the Church of Uganda. This was the confirmation of a clear call of God. For years we had been collecting material on the movement in which I had been actively involved for so long. The research into letters, articles, records and books continued with enthusiasm, and we began the writing of what was to become this rather large manuscript, which was completed by 1972 when we finally returned to England from a very disturbed Uganda with the manuscript and files of the primary material collected over the years. [Canon Ian Leakey remembered Joe as 'a man who knew the importance of keeping written records and committing to paper facts and truths without which later generations would be much the poorer'.]

The book has been highly praised – for example, by Kevin Ward of Mukono Theological college, Uganda, who described it as 'the most important autobiographical account to emerge (and unlikely to be equalled), a most useful source of information on the early days of the revival both because Dr Church was such a central figure and also because he has so meticulously preserved his journals and correspondence'. [Kevin Ward, *Obedient Rebels*, p. 195.]

This was Joe's last big achievement. Gradually his health declined and Decie had to help him more and more. She wrote, for example, in the CUMB circular letter of April 1989, 'For the last issue in October 1988 Joe was able to dictate, for me to type, messages to each one who had written. Now, especially since early January this year, the increasing disabilities of old age have caught up with him, and I am more involved in helping him in many ways, including writing this letter.'

Joe died on 29 September 1989, aged ninety, in a nursing home in Royston. Despite the hopes that her children had, of developing their relationships with her and of sharing with her some happy last years, Decie, lost without him, followed him a year-and-a-half later. She died aged eighty-six, on 30 March 1991 in a nursing home in Cirencester, near where Janine and Hugh were then living. To Janine it seemed that she died of a broken heart.

Although Joe and Decie had had to leave Gahini in 1961, and John and Rhoda not long afterwards, the work of the mission continued. Beryl Sisley, whose husband Ted came to Gahini in 1957 as director of the primary schools having done educational work in other parts of Ruanda, remembers Joe and Decie, with whom they overlapped for a few years:

Decie was gentle, I loved her. She taught me all I needed to know about gardening in Africa, pruning the citrus trees so that they produced masses of lemons, and so many other things. Joe was very particular about his car. The gardener used to polish it inside and out. Joe was practical, he taught us how to use the wood-burning stove, cutting the wood just right. He was also a man of prayer, and never made snap decisions for the sake of it. He would wait for the Holy Spirit's leading and would not rush. He had been building the *Ecole Artisinale* – a rural trade school – a lovely building to the design of another missionary, Bert Osborn. In 1963 we had to close the *Artisinale* and reopen it as a secondary school.

As Beryl remembered, things changed very much at Gahini in 1961 when not only Joe and Decie, but other Christian leaders, many of whom were Tutsi, left too. The Sisleys stayed on, running the schools until 1972 and then came back again for ten more years from 1979–89. Beryl loved Gahini and came to feel she belonged there, though spiritually it was a difficult time as materialism began to creep in. The revival flame was still alight, but burning much more quietly. Over the years the language of the revival was still used by the older Christians, and the revival formulae were still followed by many of them – repentance in the prayer meetings, the singing and dancing. David Stringer, teacher at Gisenyi Bible School from 1988, remembered, 'There was always a group of older ladies – toothless, bald – who were closer than most to the revival as well as to the old Ruandan dancing, who threw themselves into all this.' For many, it was more than a formula and the Holy Spirit was at work in their lives. But for others, especially the younger more Westernized people, it gradually lost its meaning. The Adeneys, working as doctors at Gahini in the mid 1960s, found that cheating, immorality and discrimination were prevalent. But there were shining exceptions – those who continued to 'walk in the light'.

Dr Rob Wilson and his wife Trisha worked at Gahini – he eventually as medical director, she as a physiotherapist – during the 1970s and 1980s – a time of relative peace in Rwanda. The country had become an independent republic in 1962, under a Hutu majority with Gregoire Kayibanda as its first president, then in July 1973 the army under General Habyarimana took power in a bloodless coup. Under his leadership Rwanda had some degree of stability and standards of living improved, but he abused his power and concentrated it in his own family and among Hutus from the north-west where he came from, an abuse which was to build up to horrifying results. Rob observed the changes in the hospital, in the surroundings and in the spiritual life of the people and the church:

The hospital buildings with their lovely two-tone bricks were badly in need of repair again by the 1970s, and equipment was limited. There were plans for rebuilding, but long and frustrating delays. By the time I became Medical Director in 1983, there were still differences of opinion with the local church leadership as to how the rebuilding project should proceed. The grounds were also terribly overgrown. The cost of manual labour had increased enormously. We tried to recreate Joe's beautiful 'parc' but it was too much to keep up. And a big storm in the mid-1980s demolished many of the trees. It was in many ways a wonderful time to be at Gahini. We were a large group of enthusiastic expatriate workers, with up to twenty-two people gathering on fellowship evenings. And it was still a beautiful place to be, with swimming and windsurfing on the lake.

Although in the 1970s there was a new wave of revival at Kigeme, particularly in the schools, which led to real Christian commitment among the younger people, when people reached their mid-thirties, material issues like homes, jobs and their children's places in the schools loomed very large. Gahini, with its schools, hospital, community health and agricultural projects was a prosperous area, providing education and jobs which led to a middle-class lifestyle. The projects began to be seen as providing jobs for the boys, the opportunity to own cars, etc. The enthusiastic younger Christians would meet with the older survivors from revival days in the *kazu* on Tuesday afternoons, but among the middle aged there was largely a spiritual wilderness. During this period of peace, there was prosperity and material progress, but spiritually life was largely evident only among the old and the young.

The hospital rebuilding was eventually completed in 1990, the buildings modernized and equipment updated and renewed. Much of David's and Joe's careful brickwork was covered with cement rendering as, according to the Rwandan architect, 'That was colonial – we're modern now.' With Rob as medical director and Liz Hardinge, a physiotherapist who worked at Gahini for many years, as accountant, the aim was to run it simply, cheaply and appropriately, providing a good service to the people round about. Liz and Trisha Wilson had also set up a rehabilitation centre for the disabled, where many, previously incapacitated, found new freedom in wheelchair sports, swimming and generally increased mobility. It seemed to be a time of new opportunity for the medical work at Gahini.

Then on 1 October 1990, Rwanda was invaded by Tutsis from Uganda to the north-east. For some time these Rwandans who had fled to Uganda as refugees in the late 1950s and early 1960s had dreamt of returning to their homeland. Not only were they in exile, but they were stateless, neither allowed to return to Rwanda nor to take Ugandan citizenship. By 1990, some of these had formed an offensive political organization, the Rwanda Patriotic Front (RPF), dedicated to the return of exiles to Rwanda, by force if necessary. It was they who invaded. At once there was retaliation. The civil war had begun. Although some missionaries left and Gahini was cut off for a while and there were curfews, the work of the hospital and schools carried on. Eventually on 4 August 1993 the RPF and the Rwanda Government signed a peace agreement in Arusha. In the same year John Church, revisiting Rwanda, discussed with leading Rwandan surgeons plans for an Association of Surgeons of Rwanda. Once again there seemed to be progress and hope.

No one had an inkling of the horrors to come when at 8.30 p.m. on 6 April 1994 the plane carrying President

Habyarimana and the President of Burundi was shot down as it flew into Kigali. From that moment no Tutsi or anyone who looked like a Tutsi was safe from the murderous militia gangs. Moderate Hutus and those from other groups were on the hit list too. Rob Wilson, still working at Gahini, heard the news on the radio early the next morning. Shocked, he went up to the hospital and started prayers with two minutes' silence. He then encouraged the hospital workers to work as normal and did his usual ward round, but there was much tension and many workers went home. By mid-afternoon a mob arrived inside the hospital enclosure looking for Tutsi refugees, there was fighting and staff were fully occupied tending the wounded. The house of Anatolie, the much-loved social worker and Ntaganda her husband was attacked and Anatolie was killed. Ntaganda was given refuge in the hospital until he could get away. Rob and Trisha had a chance to get away too, but decided to stay until given orders by the consul or the bishop. Then followed a terrible rerun of the events of 30 years earlier.

Next day, as Rob was operating on more wounded brought in by ambulance, a mob arrived:

They banged on the door where we were working, demanding that we open up, give them keys and allow them to take whom they wanted. I said I was unable and that we had work to do. They threatened to kill me; and then they left. We could hear them going round the hospital and looking for refugees. They found Higiro, husband of one of our nurses, and killed him and dragged him past the operating room window. There were whistles and shouting. It would have been very easy to enter the operating room and so we simply prayed – for ourselves and for the murderous mob – and then sat and waited. After about an hour the Bourgmestre arrived with a few gendarmes and the mob dispersed.

Not for long though, and the gendarmes did nothing to prevent the ensuing massacre, with a young man hacked to death right outside the window, and women and children herded out of the gates to be killed. At midday a message came from the consul advising Rob and Trisha to leave which, particularly with their children's safety in view, they decided to do. As Rob recorded, 'Leaving was extremely painful. We had not even said goodbye to our house staff who had been so calm and helpful in these difficult days and over the last ten years. We knew that a lot of the true Christians at Gahini we would never see again. And I felt guilty that in the end I had not been able to save the folk who had come to the hospital for refuge, and that I had not been prepared to choose to die with them.'

By Tuesday 12 April they were in Tanzania, where they were to work among Rwandan refugees, including some staff from Gahini hospital, in the Benaco refugee camp. At the time though they did not know this would happen and could feel only guilt. Rob wrote in his diary, 'Our Rwandan brothers and sisters have been totally abandoned. None of us stayed. None of us could cope with either of the possibilities of coping with prolonged terror or violent injury and perhaps death. The Rwandan Christians had no choice. We have tried during these years to preach and live biblical Christianity. Will our inability to take the ultimate risk negate what we have been trying to preach?'

In fact, a few days later, on 16 April, because of increasing danger both from the local militia and from the approaching RPF army, many of the Rwandan Christians left for Tanzania too, walking in family groups for mile after mile, and writing from the camp of God's goodness and grace in preserving their lives. Later, in 1997, when the refugees had been sent back to Rwanda and Rob and Trisha were shortly due to retire as missionaries after 15 years service, they hoped to put in their last few months back at

Gahini working in a voluntary capacity as reconcilers. But the hospital had been taken over by the new government, there seemed no hope (then) of the church ever running it again, and they were told they were not wanted; there was no further need for volunteers. As Rob realized, Joe Church was the first missionary doctor at Gahini and Rob was possibly the last. To his great sorrow, almost all the medical and operating records including details of Joe's earliest operations were looted from the office and lost. John Church had visited in 1990 and seen the leather-bound volume which recorded Joe's first operation in September 1929, 'incision and drainage of abcess'. Now they were lost forever.

Others too bear witness to the suffering of Rwanda. Lesley Bilinda, a TEAR Fund health worker married to a Rwandan teacher based at Gahini, was out of the country when the massacres began. Her husband, a Tutsi, fled to Butare where he was killed. Remembering the lake at Gahini as it used to be, breathtakingly beautiful at sunset with reds, gold and orange while frogs croaked and the water lapped gently on the shore, how could she think of it now with hundreds, perhaps thousands of bodies chopped up by machete and thrown into its waters? She visited beloved Rwandan Christian friends at the Benaco refugee camp – faithful believers whom she described as shining like lights, still trusting in God. As one of them said, 'We are not here because of the war. We are here because God wants to teach us something. This is God's school for us at this time. So many good and wonderful things are happening.' Lesley then went back to Gahini later in the year. The RPF were now running the country and much was changed:

My first stop was Rusi's little house. A single, elderly lady who hobbled about on crutches because she had only one leg, Rusi spent much of her time in her tiny crumbling bedroom, praying. She had become a Christian during the East Africa Revival of the 1930s, through the love and care of the Christian staff of Gahini hospital. Now, in response, she spent many hours a day alone in her little house, praying for the staff and the hospital . Her body was weak and frail, but her spirit was undaunted. She was an inspiration to be with.

The market was humming with activity again. Lesley met several people she knew, who all had tales to tell of what had befallen them and how they had survived. Then, as she wrote, reflecting unconsciously on Joe's work, 'I walked quickly round the side of the large red-brick church, and started down the hill. The beauty of the place struck me once again. Huge old trees, heavy with blossom, lined the road from the church, giving an air of permanence and stability. And yet now there was neither permanence nor stability. So much had changed . . .'

It had indeed. A soldier had taken over her and Charles's house. The garden had been used as a mass grave. Sticking out of the uneven clods of earth were human bones, skulls, bits of clothing. She was sickened to learn that her loved colleague Anatolie, like many many others throughout the country, had actually been killed by people she knew. Members of the gang who killed her lived only a few hundred yards from her home. What could one make of it all?

Many Christians, despite their firm trust in God, were killed, both Tutsi and Hutu – some even as they sought refuge in church buildings. As John Church has observed, places like churches and mission buildings which had formerly been sanctuaries, often proved to be death traps in 1994. Many others had miraculous escapes and testify to God meeting their needs for food as they were in hiding, or preserving them through unexpected kindness from friends and even strangers. Some Christians risked their lives to stand by and help. One such was the Rev Malachi Munyaneza, touched by the 1970s revival, who narrowly escaped death for giving refuge to Tutsis in his home in Kigali. Lined up by militiamen, with a pistol at his forehead and a machine gun at his ribs, he tried to explain that as a man of God he felt it important to share what he had and to give refuge to needy Tutsis: 'At that moment I felt like the wind, transparent, ready to go – only God was important.' Somehow the gang were distracted by cars being looted in the courtyard. They left, and he survived thanks to some born-again soldiers bringing him food.

Others, as we have seen, found help and Christian fellowship in the camps. David Stringer, eventually reunited with his family after much uncertainty, helped with aid work in the Goma refugee camp, using his Land-Rover to collect and deliver drugs, move bodies, get equipment for lighting and water supplies. He linked up with people he knew, including a pastor from Gisenyi, and was impressed to see how the pastors had established open-air churches in the camps, and saw them as a focus of people's getting on their feet again.

Others have found it hard to understand how such a total breakdown of civilization and morality could occur in a country which had been strongly influenced by Christianity – both by the identification of the nation with the Roman Catholic Church over many years, and by a vigorous and heartfelt Protestant revival movement. One person who has grappled with this issue, particularly as it relates to the revival, is the Rev Roger Bowen, one-time General Secretary of the Ruanda Mission, now known as Mid-Africa Ministry. (See his article 'Revivalism and Ethnic Conflict: Questions from Rwanda', *Transformation* 12, 2, April 1995. Also his J.C. Jones Lecture, *Rwanda – Missionary Reflections on a Catastrophe*, for the CMS Welsh Members' Council, 1995.)

After distinguishing between revival – a many-stranded initiative of God, and revivalism – an effort of man, Bowen praised the revival for the way in which it confronted the ethnic issue right at the outset, not in an overt or formalized way, but by bringing a white man and a black man together at the foot of the cross. He concluded that the revival at its beginning and at its best spoke very directly to the ethnic issue, in that it led to a new identity 'in Christ' where there is neither Jew nor Greek, white nor black, Hutu nor Tutsi, as demonstrated in the travelling teams of witness which were interracial, and in the fellowship meetings. He pointed out too that as ethnic conflicts arose in East Africa at the time of independence – for example, with the rise of Mau Mau in Kenya – it was often the revival brethren who had discovered a new identity in Christ who stood firm. As time went on, though, this oneness in Christ was forgotten by many. There were glorious exceptions – stories of heroic faith and courage where Christians who were also Hutu helped and protected their Tutsi neighbours from the *Interehamwe* (Hutu extremist) militias, but the future generations on the whole were less touched by genuine revival. As Bowen put it, 'Within the contemporary church situation in Rwanda the fires of revival had died down. Some would use the language of revival but often the reality was not present.' In a situation of insecurity and threat, people then readily fell back on their ethnic identity, and were wide open to exploitation by unscrupulous politicians. Roger Bowen also suggested that

... The revival background of the church in Rwanda has been strong on the evangelistic task but weak on discipleship and training, with little teaching on how to live out Christian discipleship in the secular world and how to be salt and light in society ... The challenge to repentance has usually focused on a fairly limited range of personal moral questions – lying, stealing, adultery, drunkenness. Ironically, the revival doctrine of sin underestimates the power and depth of evil, and by focusing on personal/private morality is quite inadequate to tackle the hideous strength of structural evil and corporate sin manifested in an act of genocide.

This last point is borne out by the Rev Malachi Munyaneza who, having lived through the genocide, concludes, 'The revival had a big impact in East Africa. It brought unity, social as well as spiritual. Its weakness was that it emphasized only salvation, eternal life, the kingdom of God. It tended to forget the realities of daily life. I am a child of the revival, but I realize that we must also teach the values of this life, here and now. We must address the important issues of democracy, injustice, the need for tolerance and the sharing of resources.'

Joe followed the leading of God's Holy Spirit in faithful obedience and sought to teach others to do the same. As a result, God greatly used him to bring many into the Kingdom of Heaven, and without addressing issues like race formally, he worked out the values of God's kingdom in his own life and helped others to do so too. Some, like Yona Kanamuzeyi, paid for this faithfulness with their lives. Joe's challenge must be for Christians to continue, starting daily at the cross, to apply the principles of that kingdom to this troubled world, and in particular to the troubled country of Rwanda.

In September 1997, 70 years since Joe first arrived in East Africa, an international convention was held at Gahini. The invitation leaflet bore a picture of the tent-shaped brick *kazu* with its thatch badly needing repair, and this wording:

It was in this small chapel that the first fellowship meetings were held as the Lord brought penitent believers into fellowship with God and one another, through the blood of the cross (in fact, it was not the same, but a similar *kazu* built by Joe in 1952, symbolically central and on the site of Geoffrey

Holmes's original tent). All walls fell, between Tutsis and Hutus, between blacks and whites. From this hill many teams were sent out to neighbouring nations and eventually around the world with a very simple message, the message of the unmerited favour of God offered freely to all who would sincerely follow the Lamb wherever he goes. From the beginning fellowship and walking in the light of Christ provided the context for spiritual growth and evangelism.

After referring to the horrors of the genocide, the invitation continued,

The killings are now over and it is a time for healing and repentance. The brothers and sisters in Rwanda need the encouragement of the international fellowship. This is the reason for the conference at Gahini. It seems fitting that many brothers and sisters from around the world should join in this event which will be a time of thanksgiving for what God did 65 years ago in those majestic Rwanda hills. It will also be a time to renew covenant with the Lord Jesus because many have grown cold and bewildered, and to meet the challenges of the future in the power of the risen Lord Jesus.

Over two thousand people came, among them Christians from many countries as well as Rwandans themselves. As the gospel was simply preached as in revival days, many testimonies were heard of God's miracles of preservation and of courageous faith which drove Hutus to die with their Tutsi brothers and sisters instead of failing to stand with them and so save their own lives. There was tearful repentance and joyful reconciliation.

Joe and Decie could hardly have believed what had happened to the country they had loved and served for many years. Certainly their prayer would be that once again many would walk in the light on the green hill of Gahini and throughout Rwanda, and that the light of cleansing, forgiveness and reconciliation found at the cross of Christ would shine more and more widely to a needy world.

Bibliography

Bilinda, Lesley, *The Colour of Darkness* (London: Hodder & Stoughton, 1996)

Bowen, Roger, 'Rwanda – Missionary Reflections on a Catastrophe', J.C. Jones Memorial Lecture 1995 (CMS Welsh Members' Council, 1995), *Anvil* 13, 1 (1996), pp. 33–44

Bowen, Roger, 'Revivalism and Ethnic Conflict: Questions from Rwanda', *Transformation* 12, 2 (April–June 1995), pp. 15–18

Butler, Bill, *Hill Ablaze* (London: Hodder & Stoughton, 1976)

Church, J.E., *A Call to Prayer* (London: Ruanda Mission, 1936)

Church, J.E., *Awake! An African Calling: The Story of Blasio Kigozi and his Vision of Revival* (London: Church Missionary Society, 1937)

Church, J.E., *Every Man a Bible Student* (London: Scripture Union, 1938)

Church, J.E., *Jesus Satisfies* (Croydon: Ruanda General & Medical Mission, 1946)

Church, J.E., *Jesus Satisfies?* (London: Ruanda Mission CMS, 1956)

Church, J.E., *Out of the Pit* (London: Marshall, Morgan & Scott, 1958)

Church, J.E. and others, *Forgive Them: The Story of an African Martyr* (London: Hodder & Stoughton, 1966)

Church, J.E., *William Nagenda: A Great Lover of Jesus* (London: Ruanda Mission CMS, 1974)

Church, J.E., *Quest for the Highest* (Exeter: Paternoster Press, 1981)

Coomes, Anne, *Festo Kivengere* (Eastbourne: Monarch, 1990)

Guillebaud, Lindesay, *A Grain of Mustard Seed: the Growth of the Ruanda Mission of CMS* (London: Ruanda Mission, CMS, 1960)

Harford Battersby, C.F., *Pilkington of Uganda* (London: Marshall Brothers, 1898)

Kamukama, Dixon, *Rwanda Conflict* (Kampala: Fountain Publishers, 1993)

Katarikawe, The Rev James, *The East African Revival Movement* (Thesis for MTh degree, Fuller Theological Seminary, Pasadena USA, 1975)

Lawrence, Carl, *Rwanda – A Walk through Darkness into Light* (Oregon: Vision House, 1995)

Murray, Jocelyn, *Proclaim the Good News – A Short History of the Church Missionary Society* (London: Hodder & Stoughton, 1985)

Murray-Brown, Jeremy, *Kenyatta* (London: George Allen & Unwin, 1972)

Neill, Stephen, *A History of Christian Missions. The Pelican History of the Church*, VI (London: Penguin Books, 1964)

Osborn, H.H., *Fire in the Hills* (Crowborough: Highland Books, 1991)

Osborn, H.H., *Revival – A Precious Heritage* (Winchester: Apologia Publications, 1995)

Prunier, Gerald, *The Rwanda Crisis – History of a Genocide* (Kampala: Fountain Publishers, 1995)

Ratcliff, Nora (Abridged), *The Journal of John Wesley* (London: Thomas Nelson & Sons, 1940)

Ruanda Notes: The Journal of the Ruanda Mission (Partners Together from September 1974)

St John, Patricia, *Breath of Life: the Story of the Ruanda Mission* (London: Norfolk Press, 1971)

Stanley Smith, A.C., *Road to Revival: The Story of the Ruanda Mission* (London: Church Missionary Society, 1946)

Tumwa, Tom and Mutibwa, Phares, (eds), *A Century of Christianity in Uganda, 1877–1977* (Nairobi: Uzima Press, 1978)

An Unknown Christian, *How to Live the Victorious Life* (London: Marshall, Morgan & Scott, no date)

Warren, Max, *Revival: An Enquiry* (London: SCM Press, 1954)

Wooding, Dan and Barnett, Ray, *Uganda Holocaust* (Glasgow: Pickering & Inglis, 1980)

Ward, Kevin, 'Obedient Rebels – The Relationship between the Early Balokole and the Church of Uganda – the Mukono Crisis of 1941', *Journal of Religion in Africa* 19, 3 (1989), pp. 194–227

Young, Dr Bill, *The Jigsaw* 1914–1942 (self-published, 1995)

Index

A Flame of Sacred Love
The Life of Benjamin Broomhall 1829–1911
Norman Cliff

Benjamin Broomhall, brother-in-law of Hudson Taylor, was one of the best known Christian laymen in Britain in the latter part of the nineteenth century.

As the General Secretary of the China Inland Mission he was a prominent figure in churches and at large conventions where he spoke on China and the cause of the missions. He was well known to Cabinet Ministers and members of Parliament for his uncompromising stand against the evils of slavery and the opium trade, and in his lifetime saw both evils largely eliminated.

Although he never set foot in China, Broomhall had a great influence on God's work in that land through hundreds of young people he selected and sent out, including five of his own children.

"Behind many a Christian visionary stand those whose complementary gifts of steady wisdom and practical management, under God, enable the vision to be realised. Here is the engrossing story of a husband and wife partnership playing exactly such a role. In no small measure, it was Benjamin and Amelia Broomhall who enables James Hudson Taylor's vision for the China Inland Mission to pass from dream to reality."
Rosemary Dowsett, OMF International, Conference and Training Ministry

Norman Cliff is the great grandson of Benjamin Broomhall. He has researched and written about the history of missions in China in the nineteenth and twentieth centuries, including events during the Sino-Japanese War from 1937–1945. As a minister he had pastorates in South Africa and Zimbabwe. He is now in retirement in Harold Wood, Essex.

ISBN 1-85078-328-4

**OM
publishing**

Roots and Wings
Five Generations and Their Influence
Elizabeth Goldsmith

Tracing her family from 1816, Elizabeth Goldsmith provides a fascinating insight into the lives and lasting legacies of five generations involved in missionary activity.

The story takes readers across continents, offering glimpses of North American settlers, Indian brahmins, Chinese mandarins, the beautiful scenery of Norway, a Japanese internment camp and Indonesian villages. It touches upon the birth and development of organisations such as the Student Volunteer Movement and the China Inland Mission. It also gives an understanding of the lives of previous generations, their different viewpoints and the ways in which they worked out their faith.

More than a personal history, *Roots and Wings* explores how we all have our 'roots' in our past. But the Holy Spirit gives us 'wings' to move beyond our roots so that a family 'heritage' can develop from one generation to another.

"A very valuable book [which] gives you a thirst for God and a longing to be used by Him, even if it costs something – or much."
Brother Andrew

"This is a book that I will recommend unreservedly to every member of my church."
Roger Ellis, Revelation Church, Chicester

"A mega testimony of reality and God's faithfulness that will increase your discernment and faith. Elizabeth is a wonderful woman of God whose writings have blessed thousands across the globe."
George Verwer, International Director of Operation Mobilisation

Before taking up the post of Lecturer at All Nations Christian College, Elizabeth Goldsmith worked for OMF in Indonesia, Singapore and Malaysia with her husband, Martin. They presently enjoy a travelling ministry that takes them around the world. The Goldsmiths have three children.

ISBN 1-85078-280-6

OM
publishing

Future Leader
Spirituality, Mentors, Context and Style for Leaders of the Future
Viv Thomas

Leadership is a key to success in any organisation.

All the more reason to get it right, says Viv Thomas in a book that sets out to discern the kind of leadership that is needed as we enter a new millennium.

Drawing on biblical models and organisational management research, along with personal experience of some of the evangelical world's most influential leaders, the author provides a model of leadership that is

- Driven by compassion, not obsession.
- Rooted in relationships, not systems.
- Promotes life, not self image.

If we fail in these areas, he argues, much of what we do in terms of goals, strategies, skills, mission and communication will eventually be blown away.

This stimulating and inspiring book will test all who might aspire to lead.

"In a world in which leadership is sick with power and pride, Viv Thomas shows a healthier way to lead – the Jesus way of weakness and humility, the biblical way of human inadequacy and divine grace . . . This book is much needed in our evangelical world that seems so easily seduced into celebrity and arrogance."
Eugene Petersen

"Here is a book that is eminently readable, full of godly wisdom, very obviously flowing from the heart of a man steeped in God's word. He repeatedly puts his finger exactly on the Lord's priorities and values."
Rosemary Dowsett, OMF International, Conference and Training Ministry

Viv Thomas is the International Co-ordinator of Leadership Development with Operation Mobilisation. He has a world-wide preaching and teaching ministry, with an emphasis on developing leaders. He is also a visiting lecturer at All Nations Christian College in Hertfordshire.

ISBN 0-85364-949-9

paternoster press